TRIUMPH
OVER
MARCOS

Triumph Over Marcos

by THOMAS CHURCHILL

A story based on the lives of
GENE VIERNES & SILME DOMINGO
Filipino American
Cannery Union organizers,
their assassination,
and the trial that followed.

OPEN HAND PUBLISHING INC.
Seattle, Washington

Copyright 1995 © Thomas Churchill

Books by Open Hand Publishing Inc. are available
through our primary distributor:

THE SUBTERRANEAN COMPANY, INC.
P.O. Box 160, 265 S. 5th, Monroe, OR 97456
Toll free orders 800-274-7826 / fax 503-847-6018

For personal orders and catalogs, please write to:

OPEN HAND PUBLISHING INC.
P.O. Box 22048, Seattle, WA 98122

Edited by Deborah Kaufmann
Cover Design by Art & Design Services, Seattle, WA
Cover photograph by John Stamets

Library of Congress Cataloging-in-Publication Data

Churchill, Thomas.
  Triumph over Marcos : a true story based on the lives of Gene Viernes and Silme Domingo, Filipino American cannery union organizers, their assassination and the trial that followed / by Thomas Churchill. -- 1st ed.
      p.   cm.
  Includes bibliographical references and index.
  ISBN 0-940880-52-0
  1. Trade-unions--Cannery workers--Washington (State)--Seattle.
2. Viernes, Gene, d. 1981. 3. Domingo, Silme, d. 1981. 4. Filipino
Americans--Employment--Washington (State)--Seattle.   I. Title.
HD6515.C27C48   1994
331.88′1640282′09797772--dc20   94-47968
                                                                     CIP

FIRST EDITION
FIRST PRINTING
Printed in the United States of America

99 98 97 96 95   6 5 4 3 2 1

NATIONAL
ENDOWMENT
FOR ❤ THE   This project is supported by a grant from the
A R T S   National Endowment for the Arts.

To the memory of

SILME DOMINGO

GENE VIERNES

—we say to them:

"Remember, remember,
We shall no longer wear rags, eat stale bread, live in darkness;
We shall no longer kneel on our knees to your false gods;
We shall no longer beg you for a share of life.
Remember, remember,
O remember in the deepest midnight of your fear,
We shall emulate the wonder of our women,
The ringing laughter of our children,
The strength and manhood of our men
With a true and honest and powerful love!

An we say to them:
"We are the creators of a flowering race!"

I say I want the wide American earth.
I say to you, too, sharer of my delights and thoughts,
I say this deathless truth,
And more—

        For look, watch, listen
With a stroke of my hand I open the dawn of a new world,
Lift up the beautiful horizon of a new life;
All for you, comrade and my love.

Carlos Bulosan, *I Want the Wide American Earth*

TABLE OF CONTENTS

FORWARD

Fourteen years have passed since Gene and my brother, Silme, were assassinated. They were very special, not only to their families, but to all of those with whom they came into contact in their struggle to make the world a better place for all people. It was clear that this was no ordinary murder. Silme and Gene were still only in their twenties when their lives were taken specifically because of the success of their work in bringing an end to corruption in the Alaska cannery union and in the Philippines. It was their determination and their success that turned them into working-class heroes. Today each of us is still confronted with decisions not unlike the ones that Silme and Gene had to make. I hope that you will be challenged and inspired by their message.

Love, murder, conspiracy, and international intrigue—these are prime elements for a book or a movie. Those of us who were close to Silme and Gene wanted the whole world to know their story. My family was approached by several writers and filmmakers. However, it wasn't until we came to know Tom Churchill in 1988 that we felt confident we had found a writer with the commitment, politics, and sincerity to write OUR book. I choose to call this OUR book because this story is the work of many people who opened their hearts in order to share with Tom their recollections of Silme and Gene. These stories made it possible for Tom to capture Silme's and Gene's characters with great clarity. I can testify that the telling of these stories brought back memories almost too difficult to deal with, even after all of these years.

While this book focuses on the lives of Gene and Silme, it is also the story of so many young Filipino Americans who looking for their identity found it in the social movement centered around the *Union of Democratic Filipinos* (KDP). Hundreds of young Filipino Americans were impacted by the work of the *KDP* and, even today, college-age Filipino Americans are curious about its history and legend. Youth are still searching for their identity and a direction for their lives, just as we were back then.

Too often peoples' struggles, especially those of a progressive nature which end in victories, are kept from the public eye and excluded from history books. The Domingo and Viernes families and the people who comprised the *Committee for Justice for Domingo and Viernes* will be forever indebted to Tom Churchill for his having immortalized our struggle.

I would like to thank everyone that participated in the making of this book. In particular, Rhonda Oden Gossett, my dear friend who knowing that this story needed to be told, suggested the book project to Anna Johnson of Open Hand Publishing. And, of course, Open Hand for its commitment to telling the history of people of color, and without which this book and other significant books might never be published.

Cindy Domingo
Seattle, Washington
February 1995

PREFACE

In 1985 while interviewing Seattle attorney John Caughlan about another Washington state labor-related murder, the Law Case in the 1930s, he mentioned several striking similarities to the June 1981 murders of Filipino American cannery union reformers, Silme Domingo and Gene Viernes. I was intrigued by the tale of their assassination, yet at the same time reluctant to take it on as a book project because of its historic immediacy. Although Tony Dictado, Jimmy Ramil, and Ben Guloy were already in prison for the actual killings, the important conspiracy case had yet to be tried. Still, I remained interested; and when, in 1988, I interviewed Silme's widow, Terri Mast, and his sister, Cindy Domingo, I became convinced their story had to be told.

The problem with all historical material—whether from the distant or the immediate past—has to do with finding the proper voices, points of view, and language to tell the tale. My favorite writing arena is the intense use of imagination, whether poetry, drama or historical fiction; the fact that Silme Domingo and Gene Viernes were vilified, threatened, and murdered by powerful forces raises them to the place usually afforded mythology. Since I find the novel generally to be more moving than pure history, I've opted for fiction to recount this piece of history. Although the dialogue can only be imagined, each event in the book is either something that did take place or could have taken place. A few names have been changed.

Every scene in which Silme or Gene appears comes from an impulse in my sources: if in the book Gene's half-brother, Glen Rabena, says, "I never think of myself as being Filipino," I can't be certain he used these words in conversation with Gene; nevertheless, he said just that in an interview with me. Glen's words might be taken as interesting self-analysis in the context of an interview, but when put in an imagined conversation between Gene and Glen—whom Gene admired as a free spirit—the remark helps the reader understand an important distinction between the two brothers. Unlike Silme, whose parents were both born in the Philippines, Gene's mother was Irish and he was often in a position—according to his siblings—of "passing," that is, of seeming white, should he choose. Nevertheless, as Gene Viernes matured he found that his own experience of cannery work was dominated by underprivileged Filipino workers who suffered under Marcos's rule; and he needed to become more, rather than less, Filipino. Gene's trip to the Philippines, as enacted in this book, is based upon research and anecdote provided by several of his friends.

Silme was the perfect counterpart to his farm-raised buddy, Gene. Urbane, academically achieving, raised on politics, Silme loved fancy clothes and cars, and was an obsessive poker player and frequenter of bars. When placed side by side, it was as though the two young men were throwbacks to classical times, but which one more resembled Don Quixote, and which one Sancho Panza, is hard to say. Both were earthy and both tilted at windmills.

My point regarding Silme and Gene, however, is not merely that they were "fascinating" and led "story book lives." They worked beyond the call of duty, whether regarding their union activity or high-level organizing. They put themselves on the line politically within a social context and during a time when to do so meant risking one's life. Once they had stepped from the relatively safe place of being union officers to adopting a platform of union reform— even to the point of insisting that all hiring in the canneries be done on a seniority basis—they risked confrontation with gambling interests that had held sway over Alaska unions for decades. The idea of running a reform policy was not nearly as dangerous, however, as combining that aim with denouncing Ferdinand Marcos, martial law, and every aspect of Marcos's dictatorship which daily eroded the lives and values of Filipinos overseas and in the United States.

As union people, Silme and Gene could not have operated alone, and would not have wanted to appear separate from the many vital organizations they helped to form. The first of these, after Local 37 of the Inland Boatman's Union, was the *Katipunan ng Demokratikong* or, loosely translated, the *Union of Democratic Filipinos*. In the book, I explain what this organization meant to Silme and Gene and hundreds of other Filipino Americans who rallied around its goals, foremost among them to bring down the reign of Ferdinand and Imelda Marcos.

Silme and Gene are probably best understood not only in the context of the organizations they embraced, but in their closeness to their families and friends as well. From my initial contact with Terri Mast and Cindy Domingo to interviews with Rene Cruz and Gelina Aliva in the Bay Area, I've been given ample information and straightforward accounts of what it was like to know and work with Silme and Gene.

Finally, though I devote this story to the lives and work of two remarkable young men and those close them, it has never been my goal to "blame" anyone or institution for their deaths. The fact of Marcos's extraordinary evil is so evident, so palpable, and already so well documented that it hardly matters to this story that we crouch over blood stains and say, "Right here, this part is Marcos's doing," or the fault of gambling interests, or Tony Baruso, or what have you. These matters have long been taken up and dealt with by the courts. What I'm interested in is the way Gene and Silme, their families, friends, and colleagues lived their lives and stood on the front line.

It's easy to wonder why our democracy has such a penchant for right-wing dictatorships. If one wishes to seek governmental blame for atrocities, how much more germane to Marcos's rule could one get than to note the way in which, one year after Marcos declared martial law in the Philippines, the Nixon administration and the CIA backed the 1973 coup in Chile, which left Salvadore Allende murdered and General Pinochet in power. Pinochet's example in arming and protecting Michael Townley—who, with two Cuban agents, murdered Orlando Letelier by means of a car bomb in Washington, DC—became the precedent by which the Domingo-Viernes conspiracy trial against the Marcos estate can be viewed. There's no end to blame, but this need not be emphasized in a story of triumph, which is what Silme and Gene were all about.

Thomas Churchill
Whidby Island, WA
February 1995

ACKNOWLEDGMENTS

In years of interviewing people I was never so rewarded by the consistent willingness of those close to Silme Domingo and Gene Viernes to give the freshest, most honest insights into their working lives. Among the Viernes family I was helped greatly in the making of the book by interviews with Gene's mother Betty Viernes, his sisters Barbara Viernes and Patty Haywood, brothers Stan and Steve Viernes, and Glen Rabena. Of his friends, I was supported and guided by Andy Pasqua, Bob Santos, Geline Aliva, and Rene Cruz.

Silme's widow, Terri Mast, and his sister, Cynthia Domingo, gave me much interview time, besides follow-up phone conversations, clarifications, and critiques, that this book would not have been possible without them. Besides these two, I was given invaluable interview time with John Caughlan, Bruce Ocena, Silme's mother Ade Domingo, his brother Nemesio Domingo, Michael Withey, and Michael Woo. Silme's sister Vangie Keefe and her husband Rich offered valuable reading critiques, not to mention a fair amount of back patting and hand holding.

Finally, most helpful among the many who guided me through the book's innumerable changes was my editor, Deborah Kaufmann. To Deborah and Anna Johnson, publisher of Open Hand, I owe a special debt of gratitude.

PART I

Seattle and Alaska
Summer 1971

Gene Viernes and Silme Domingo met for the first time outside Local 37 of the Inland Boatman's Union, as they angled for the same parking space. Silme pulled his slick Monte Carlo ahead, and Gene drove his grubby Luv truck behind and halfway into the open space. By the time they finished yelling at one another, they realized they had at least the union and cannery work in common. It was the end of the summer leading into Silme's first year at the University of Washington. Both men had just returned from Alaska.

Gene would never admit that Silme was the first Filipino he'd encountered who was going to the university. Silme, without meaning to, made him feel like a hick. Maybe it was his smile, somewhere between wise guy and friendly, or his way of using street slang that threw Gene off. Silme was hefty and taller than Gene, but Gene seemed bigger, standing frankly straight, carrying his wrestler's body loose and easy, ready to work or dribble a basketball passed by one of his Yakima Valley buddies down the court to lay it in. Gene was a natural athlete and could take apart and put back together anything mechanical. He was always reading—about machines, politics, labor history, literature. Silme was more naturally intellectual, but after their first conciliatory cup of coffee together in the union cafeteria, each had one comment for the other: "That guy's got brains."

❧

In the following summer of 1971, Gene and Silme were reacquainted in the Anchorage International Airport on their trip back to the canneries. Gene had just graduated from high school,

3

while Silme had finished his freshman year at the university. A shorter flight would take Silme to the New England Fish Company's cannery at Uganik Bay on Kodiak Island; Gene and his friend, Andy Pascua, would fly on to King Salmon in Bristol Bay, where a bus would take them and the rest of their Wapato, Washington, crew to a Wards Cove plant at Red Salmon.

The airport bar was filled with college students, older Asian men and women and, as usual, a whole clutch of new arrivals from the Philippines, work-fodder for the canneries. A mass of leather-jacketed men sat around a table near the bar, dark bushy permed heads leaning in over gold neck chains and a blaze of tropical shirts. The men were playing hi que, a domino-like game played with ivory tiles that resembled those used in mahjong. Shouts of Tagalog and Ilocano dialects augmented the clacking tiles. Played in the cannery dormitories, hi que busted some workers so thoroughly they owed more than their paychecks to the foreman at the end of each week.

Silme took a seat between Gene and Andy, his eyes on the game players. Wearing a blue work shirt and worn jeans, he was bigger than Gene but softer. Dark shadows under his eyes aged an otherwise young and lively face. "Hey, guys, new year, same scene—what do you say, Gene?"

"Silme, good to see you. My best buddy, Andy—"

"Pascua." Andy spoke so quietly Silme had to lean toward him to hear. He and Silme amply filled their chairs and resembled one another until Andy smiled, revealing a wide gap between his front teeth, and Silme reached for his glasses to better study the hi que players.

They watched quietly for a moment, mesmerized by the click of tiles in the men's hands. Cries of triumph and disappointment cut through a haze of cigarette smoke. Silme asked his companions, "Do you remember any of those guys?"

"Just as soon forget them," Gene said. "How was your year at the U?"

"Still shell-shocked from finals week. Not bad, though. How'd you do?"

Andy rose. "Got to take a leak," he pleaded. "Two beers on the plane, now this local moose piss. Later."

"School talk gets to him," Gene explained. "I didn't do too bad." He wasn't used to bragging, and knowing that Silme had gone to the University of Washington made him more leary, the way he felt with all people from Seattle. But he spilled out his recent life: his lightweight championship at the state meet, a few good grades, junior college in the fall.

"Terrific," Silme said. He leaned back in the seat. Rain beat against the bay windows behind him and fifty miles to the west, the Chugach Range brooded under caps of snow.

"Did you bring foam this time?" Gene asked.

"What?" Silme stared at him.

"I brought a roll of foam. It's only a half-inch thick, but it's better than those rock mattresses."

Silme laughed. "I thought you meant the foam women use." It was Gene's turn to stare. "For not getting pregnant," Silme added. Gene's face reddened. "That's okay, man. I'm sure what you brought makes more sense."

They both laughed, not a little grimly, as they remembered those forever damp bunks in the cannery dorm. Though the work was welcome, the conditions had always been harsh. Filipino women were stuck in bunkhouses eight to a room; dorms for all others allowed two. Filipinos and Alaska Natives were housed in old wooden barracks. Cracks in the siding in Gene's dorm at Red Salmon were large enough to see through. There were two different mess halls, and separate menus for whites and non-whites. Owners offered no refrigeration for food in the Filipino barracks. White barracks had washers and dryers, while Filipino barracks had wringer washers and clothes hooks. Filipinos washed their sheets and hung them on nails to dry.

Silme looked over at the men playing hi que. "I wonder if anyone told them what they're going to do up here besides gamble."

"Who hired them?" Gene asked.

"Navarro." Silme named their union dispatcher, a member of the old guard who devoted himself to gambling bosses in Seattle's International District.

"Say no more." Gene nodded. "So how was your year?"

"Not too bad."

Gene thought Silme might be holding back because school had been difficult for him. Finally Silme added, "I had a couple of Bs."

"That's not bad for first year," Gene blurted out.

Silme laughed. "No, I mean those were my only Bs."

"Fucking brain."

"They love us on that campus, man. We're the newest minority on the rise."

"Give me a break."

5

"No, you'll see." Silme laughed again and said mockingly, "Well, here come the Filipinos. What can we do for them?"

None of the Filipinos in Wapato, the Central Washington fruit-growing community where Gene had grown up, ever went to college. Gene felt self-conscious with Silme, afraid he might say the wrong thing.

"The best class I took," Silme said, "was about Marxism and Darwin. It was the only upper-division class I tried, and I aced it."

"Marxism?" Gene stumbled on the word.

"Karl Marx. What you don't get taught in Wapato, probably, no?" He laughed again. "What do you study down there, potatoes I and II? I never been on a farm."

"You got a lot to learn. We'd sweat your butt off, driving those loser trucks of Mr. Torres into town at five in the morning to pick up the winos, working goddamn Yakima hop fields, 110 degrees. Get you in shape." Gene poked Silme in the gut.

"You talked me out of it. Anyway, I'll sweat enough up here. I may be pretty soft right now, but after that first double shift I'll be a skinny ghost. Where you working? Red Salmon? I'm in Kodiak again, nothing there but that stinking cannery. At least my brother's coming up in a week."

"This summer's going to fly by," Gene said, "unless they bug us too much. If they piss us off, they better remember there're a lot of us up here this summer. We got a whole crew from Wapato."

"You're lucky. There's just me, my brother, and my cousin at Uganik Bay."

"They'd better not push us. Last year I had a big Coke stain on my sheet and when I went to supply to exchange it, the asshole clerk pointed at a pile of yellow scraps, like used diapers. When I asked for the supervisor, his eyes swelled up. 'I want those sheets,' I told him, 'the white ones, sucker, not the thin yellow ones a toenail can razor open.'"

"That's the way you have to treat that shit." Silme nodded his head approvingly. "We all start protesting, we could bring this place down."

"Maybe. Tell me more about college."

"I talk enough I might convince you to go to a good school," Silme kidded.

"Naw, I'm going to wrestle for Yakima Community College, get a free ride," Gene said, but his voice trailed off as if he himself wasn't entirely convinced.

"Whatever turns you on," Silme told him. "My best class was in political science, with an instructor who travels back and forth to the Philippines." He watched the hi que players warily. "Anti-Marcos like you wouldn't believe. And I took my first undergraduate course in Labor Econ. Studied the Wagner Act that came under Roosevelt's administration. A real important law," Silme pointed out, "the one that allows a worker to strike."

"We got stuff in our family that's like history, too."

"Yeah? No kidding?"

Suddenly one of the players Silme knew only as Jimmy was standing over them. Jimmy had come from Manila the year before, maintaining alliances with other new arrivals rather than Filipino Americans.

"Silme, how's it going, mon?" Lean and wiry, Jimmy brushed cigarette smoke from his eyes and put out his hand.

"Hey, man, what's happening? You know Gene?"

"Sure, I know Gene." Jimmy's street accent was cool, pushing open a space in which to operate.

Gene couldn't remember meeting this guy with the sharked-back hair. Ramil's saying that he knew him caused sweat to cool upon his neck. "How's it going, you ready to work?" Gene asked casually, trying to gain the upper hand. He was certain he didn't know this man, but suspected he was as evil as he looked. Jimmy mocked surprise. "Work? Sure. I come up, didn't I? Long plane ride for nothin', man." He yelled in Tagalog at the men playing hi que, and they glanced at Silme and Gene and laughed. He touched Silme's shoulder. "Hey, tell your sister no hard feelings, you know what I mean?"

"I'm sure she can speak for herself," Silme said.

The man stared at Silme, then toward the bar. "She gonna speak to me? She's kinda cute. Where is she, at the bar? She with those chicks in the other room?"

"No, she's not here. You're here. She got bumped. But she still might make it up this summer. People get sent back." Silme stopped and looked easily at the guy. "People get injured—"

"Oh, I see. Somebody gonna get hurt?"

"It happens," Gene said, finishing for Silme, wanting to be rid of the man. "People get in trouble. Whoever's next on the list knows to stay ready."

"Ah, but there's strawberries and peas for her to pick on the farm."

7

"Oh, no, she can pull roe, she can weigh, she can fill with anybody up here. She's already been here. She'll be back."

"Chicks are better in the fields, like back home," he said.

"I doubt it," Silme interrupted. Jimmy dismissed them with a chop of his hand and headed back to his game.

"Let's walk." Silme glanced back as he moved towards the door. "Class traitor, huh? Perfect example."

Gene nodded. "A real coconut."

They pushed open the door into a waiting area crowded with people talking and sleeping. Two young women, college-aged, wearing worn flannel shirts and jeans were laughing over a slick magazine. A Filipina rested fitfully on her duffel bag. One old woman ate with her fingers from a container of rice while another drank tea from a thermos.

Silme sat next to a young woman reading the *Seattle Post-Intelligencer*. She looked up and smiled. Oval eyes and high-slanted cheekbones were framed by folds of dark hair tucked into a red bandanna. She pointed to the paper. "Marcos is stealing the country blind, that's what this guy says."

"It's true. But look at this powerhouse we got here, sister," Silme said.

"I thought your sister got bumped by that creep Jimmy?"

Silme and the woman grinned. "Naw, I just call Melia my sister, actually she's my cousin." The three of them laughed. "Gene won the state championship in wrestling," Silme told her.

Melia raised her thin eyebrows. "Maybe you can kick ass with some of our beauty parlor workers in the bar."

"Maybe they'll all die of hair spray."

"Maybe the sun will shine. Fat chance. Rained three nights out of five, isn't that what we counted last June?" Silme asked Melia.

"Something like that. Just let me get the job done, grab my pay, and head to the sun."

"Seattle?" Gene asked.

"Hell no. Someplace good and hot, maybe Hawaii. Just swim and lie on the beach."

Silme threw back his head and crowed, "Sun beating down, girls in bikinis!" He grabbed Gene's hand. "Let's go!"

"Great idea, Silme, but already on the plane I was dreaming of the line. I see salmon coming toward me. And our Wapato crew: Andy, his brother, John, then his dad and another older guy; we look like ramparts in a fort. My dad, Felix, is up in the balcony somewhere. Then the Iron Chink appears and my brother, Stan, his hands freezing in salt water, sliding gutted fish across the metal table. I'm hustling racks of cans into the mouth of a retort. Suddenly I hear the owner yelling at Stan, something about too much weight on the table, and my dad comes flying off the balcony like Tarzan and lights into the guy."

Silme and Melia were nodding with him as though they'd had the same dream, or similar ones. "My dream was as real as the night Stan's hands went numb last summer—I'll never forget his screams. My dad grabbed his hands and blew on them until the feeling came back." Gene grimaced. "Sometimes I think I'm lucky to be up here, other times I'm scared I'll have this job the rest of my life—the way my dad must have felt."

"I'll tell you a story," Silme said. "Last year, when I first got to Uganik Bay, I prowled through one of the old dorms, just before it was torn down. Carved on one of the bunks I see, 'Nemesio Domingo, 1927.' My dad. He's a manong, came over here with one of the first waves of Filipino workers. He'd still be coming up if he hadn't been disabled in World War II."

No one spoke. Then Silme asked, "You ever been to the Philippines, Gene?"

"No, but I want to. I got relatives in Manila."

"When?"

Gene laughed cautiously. "Maybe in a few years. Right now it's about as tempting as Nam."

Silme frowned.

Melia explained for her cousin. "Silme's lottery number's two; he's just sick—"

Silme waved her off, having worried enough over Vietnam. "Things could be worse. I'm lucky I got my family," he maintained. "Most of us get along good. But my dad's ex-military and when it comes to Nam, we got nothing to say. He's even worse on Marcos."

"Don't tell me."

The three remained quiet for a long time. It was hard not to think of the old days, what it must have been like coming to this country, working in the hop fields, the pea harvests, picking apples in Wenatchee, hoofing it to Alaska by steamer, all your money spent on the ticket. Working under a system that allowed your labor to be contracted to a cannery for years, the beatings when you started to do well. Gene told Silme and Melia his father's story of the decent white teacher who drove around to Yakima fruit-picking camps to teach Filipinos how to read. When she was found out, the workers, including his dad, were beaten by vigilantes.

"Sounds like your dad has read Carlos Bulosan," Melia said.

"Who?"

"Bulosan, my favorite writer," Silme explained. "He wrote for our union. You didn't know that? The teacher's in one of his stories. I'll give you the book. Not that it couldn't have happened to your dad, too. You ought to meet some of those old guys like Bulosan, threatened with deportation in the fifties just for organizing."

Just then Andy moved in from the bar. "Hey, Gene, grab your duffel. Plane's leaving in five minutes."

❖

Gene and Andy had begun working at the Red Salmon cannery when they were sixteen; coming to Alaska was an adventure then. Now they stepped off the bus into the odor of tidal mud. The stink of fish guts hit them next, then the shrieking of the Iron Chink, a machine invented early in the century to mechanize the butchering of fish and replace Chinese cannery workers. They slogged up the muddy path to the dormitories with their crew lined behind them, past warehouses and storage buildings, stretching into the water on barnacled pilings. The buildings of the cannery all looked alike, as though the US Army's World War II presence had never been eradicated.

Reuniting with Silme affected Gene more deeply than he knew at first. From his first trip north, he had seen that Asian and Alaska Native cannery workers were treated differently from whites but after meeting Silme, experiencing those differences made him more angry than resigned. He had always known that what they were being fed was substandard compared to the food served in the white mess, but now he tasted the difference with every bite. As he and his co-workers talked and played their boombox in their bunkhouse, he felt the alteration creeping over him.

In one short meeting, Silme's ideas had broadened Gene's own shoulders, as if preparing him to take this place by the lapels and demand, "Where do you get off, fucking with us?" When he spoke with the women who weren't exhausted by overtime, who weren't afraid of breaking company warnings against communicating with non-white workers, he wanted to ask, "What right have they to tell us who we can talk to?" In the 1930s, a white woman could lose her

10

citizenship if she married a Filipino; Gene's mother had done it twice in a later decade and suffered the scorn of her Irish family. Gene felt his father's fight—though he knew he did not want to live his father's life over again.

Early in the summer the Alaska Department of Fish and Game put a hold on fishing, as not enough salmon were showing up. To make work, the company bosses had Gene and his Wapato friends clean the bunkhouses, ordering them to stack footlockers in the air and then take them down to make sure conditions were "sanitary," the foreman told them. The young men wondered why conditions didn't need to be sanitary before they arrived, and noticed the way the white workers in charge shouted out their instructions with precision, as though making sure their English was understood.

Below the cannery entrance, cliffs two hundred feet high and covered with long grass hung over the bay. The bosses decided the grass looked unsightly, and devised a system of ropes that ran off a cable embedded in concrete and rock at the top of the cliffs. From the cable were tie-offs which Gene, Andy, and their brothers, Stan and John, attached around their waists. Armed with machetes, the men descended the cliffs, their bodies at a thirty-degree incline to the slope. Andy thought it exhilarating to discover huge birds' nests with fresh dung inside, and spot a gray whale shooting water from its blowhole. But late in the afternoon, when Gene's foot slipped on the slick grass and he fell on his stomach, the wind kicked out of him, he took a long time to stretch the proper angle back into his body.

At the end of a long day of cutting grass and looking down into the blue sea, Gene and the others climbed back up to the main cable. Andy hit the cable hard with his machete. "Will you look at that—this machete's strong enough to cut a couple strands."

"Let me try." Gene hit the cable harder and more strands sprung loose. Then Stan took a turn, and John, biggest of them all, cut fiercely. After reducing the cable to a third its original size, they sought out the foreman. "Jeez, we're sorry, but we kind of messed up your cable." As the foreman climbed through the neck-high brush, they could hear him cursing steadily.

When the salmon returned, Gene's crew went back to working shifts, moving through a period of production so demanding that the younger men took speed in order to stay up all night. When the pace grew too hectic, they hid the older men against the wall with sacks over their heads. In this way they survived peak periods and their fathers and uncles avoided exhaustion. Gene stopped thinking of the hours he was putting in, a mechanical drone, his mind ticking rather than thinking.

One night Gene asked a machine operator where he had gotten the piece of chocolate cake he was eating. "I got it in the mess," the man said, licking frosting from his fingers. Gene grabbed Andy and the two of them walked into the white mess. "We'd like some cake," Gene told the cook, "maybe six or seven pieces."

The cook shook his jowls and hooked his thumbs into his greasy apron. "No way."

"What do you mean? You serve cake here but you won't serve it to us? Why not?" Gene pressed.

The cook whipped off his apron and squeezed it in his fist. "It's not on your goddamn menu! You got your own mess!"

"Fuck that," Andy said quietly, intimidating with his bulk. "Give us the cake."

"Hey, take it up with the owners. They set the rules around here."

"What rules? The rules got to be wrong, don't they, if they give cake to these guys—" Gene pointed at several white workers grinning over their coffee, acting entertained "—and not to us? What are we supposed to eat?"

"Well, whatever you eat!" The cook's hairy neck was turning a deep red.

"Well, what do we eat, asshole?" Andy yelled, surprising even Gene with his fury.

The cook's hand passed over a cleaver as he sidled to the exit. "That's it, you two. Hey, Tony, Al! You're my witnesses—I didn't do nothing here but follow the menu, and I'm being hassled, ain't I?"

"Where is the goddamn cake?" Gene moved toward him.

As the cook ran out he screamed, "In the goddamn reefer, big shot, and you guys' ass is grass!"

Gene and Andy hefted a big flat of cake back to the other mess hall. Soon everybody in their bunkhouse, frosting spread over their faces, was congratulating them. Felix, however, took a bite, wiped his mouth and took a long look at Gene, as if thinking his son had taken a step he might never be able to retrace.

Gene and Andy didn't get fired, but the owners did not change the menu, either. The food got worse. They served more tired ginger beef, shiny green on the edges. "Chow mein," they called it, but most of the Wapato crew had never seen chow mein, except in the Luck Toy Restaurant in Toppenish, and they never ordered it there, either. Finally Gene lost patience and announced to everyone in the dormitory that he was going on a hunger strike.

"A hunger strike? You mean you just don't eat?" Andy's gap-toothed smile faded fast. "Jesus Christ, I guess I got to go along with you." He called to the others, "Crazy Gene's going on a hunger strike, anyone else want to go along?"

❉

On the first night of their strike, ten workers ordered as much food as possible and ate until stuffed. The next night they walked into the mess but didn't eat a bite. They took all the food—the portions now increased because of the amount they'd eaten the night before—and threw it in the garbage. Then they ate platefuls the next night, demanding even more. On the following night again they refused to eat. The cooks were furious; management was getting the word.

Gene

Eight nights no nine my ribs sticking into the mattress what was I dreaming those voices again outside the window Gene Gene come down to the water the fish want you the fish the eagles calling fly with us Gene fly far out over the ice damn it's hot I need water where's that water this blanket is suffocating.

Finally the company owner called Gene into his office. His face was the color of pink meat. "We need you at your full strength, Gene, you're one guy I really value up here. You want to change messes, is that it? Personally I don't give a shit, but these goddamn food games are getting on everyone's nerves. Everyone's talking about it and that causes big problems in morale, big problems in production. We're at peak season right now, so what do you say, you want an apple, an orange? Tell me what you want, stud, because frankly you are pissing me off big time. If you was just Joe Blowhole, you'd be out of here on the first plane, but you are one of my very best, so

13

why don't we just shape the fuck up here, okay, Gene? I've already called Mr. Navarro back at your union and he is very upset. If I call him again, you can't imagine how upset he'll be. Coffee? Yes? Cream?"

"I don't want any goddamn coffee."

"It's not 'goddamn' coffee, it's damn good coffee."

"It's food. Today, we're off it."

"Be a hard guy, then," the owner said. He pointed to the door and reached for the phone.

❀

When the season ended Gene spent a week in Seattle before going home to pack for college. Finished with work, he could enjoy the bonus of having pocket money and a big city to roam. He spent time in the Public Market and downtown parks, feeling the appeal of Seattle's diverse ethnicity on Second Avenue, Occidental Street and the Asian markets and hotels in the International District. He discovered a comradeship with the most desperate alcoholics, giving them whatever change he had in his pockets.

Gene ran into Silme again and this time felt less naive, more brotherly toward him. Silme brought him to his house in Ballard and inside its tidy brick walls, Gene coveted the warmth created by his friend's large Filipino family. Crosses and other Catholic symbols unfamiliar to Gene adorned the walls, and an enormous family portrait, taken when Silme was in high school, graced the end of one room. In the photo Silme stood over his older brother, Nemesio Jr., and three sisters wearing bouffant hairstyles and dresses cut above their knees.

They sat at the kitchen table, drinking tea. Outside, Mrs. Domingo's garden was heavy with tomatoes and zucchini. Gene asked Silme about his summer. Silme lifted his hands, palms up. "You didn't hear?"

"Rumors," Gene said.

"They're true. Nemesio and I are blacklisted. We found out when we got home. We had to guess at the reasons, but it's standard procedure with New England Fish. We listened to workers' complaints because we were shop stewards, then passed them on. NEFCO management told us we were 'wise guys.' What about you?"

Gene told him about the hunger strike.

"I already heard," Silme said. "I don't think they're going to want

14

you back at Red Salmon, either."

Gene agreed. "I already figured that out, talking to Navarro. Maybe I can get other work in the summer, no?"

"Screw the canneries. Who needs to be alaskeros?" Silme said. Then the conviction came back into his voice. "Maybe we'll sue them for discrimination—what do you think about that?"

"That's a joke, right?"

"Is that what your hunger strike was?"

"No. They messed with us, and we had them real pissed off. But how do you sue a cannery?"

"You organize, gather some evidence, start a class action. It's been done with other work. Nobody's tried it here, even though we know they're discriminating. It's the damn distance that scares people, and the absolute hold the canneries have. But Alaska is a state, and we're citizens."

"You get a lawsuit going, I'll testify against Wards Cove," Gene promised.

❉

Silme fixed Gene up with a date, a last-minute choice. They doubled with Silme and his girlfriend, Shari Woo, whose lively eyes shone from an oval face. Gene's date, Molly, was a white woman, taller than he, who had recently arrived from Montana. She told him she wanted to take him there. "A fruit farm's nothing compared to a real ranch," she scoffed. At Mandarin Garden on Jackson Street, the foursome ordered five dishes plus extra rice and San Miguel beer. Silme moved his hand skillfully over the menu, showing them what to eat and what to avoid. Gene worried about the choice of restaurant after their experience in the cannery, but Silme assured him that comparing real Chinese food to what the cannery served was like comparing fresh salmon to canned.

Later, when both men went off to the restroom, Shari addressed Molly, whom she also had met for the first time that evening. "How do you like Seattle?"

"Ask me something easier."

"What do you think of Gene?" Shari tried.

Molly glanced behind her, then studied the menu. "I don't think he likes me. Acted pissed when I lit a smoke. And quiet! Is he really Filipino? He doesn't look it."

"You mean, he's not dark like Silme?"

"I don't mean it matters! I put my foot in it, sorry."

"Don't worry," Shari assured her. "If Gene doesn't talk, you can always count on Silme."

"Yeah, he seems nice. What's he like?"

"He's serious, but fun. It's all mixed with Silme, the personal, the politics. He talks to everybody—old, young, square, hip, redneck. He's going to the U to get a degree, then he'll work down here in the International District. We tutor Chinese and Filipino immigrant kids at our drop-in center. I started hanging out here when I was nineteen; my dad was a lodge member and the ID's my backyard."

In the men's room, Silme asked his friend, "What do you think?"

"Yeah, that Shari's something else."

Silme's eyes widened at Gene's misplaced eagerness. "No kidding—and we're crazy about each other."

The restaurant was crowded, mostly with Asians. As the men returned to their table, Silme pointed across the room. The cannery worker they'd met in the Anchorage airport was sitting with gambling boss Tony Dictado, a union foreman, and two others Gene knew as gang members. Jimmy was dressed in a blue silk shirt, gold beaming off his chest and wrists.

Silme and Gene stared at each other as they sat down to the remains of a fish and garlic lobster sauce dinner. "Did you hear what that joker did?" Silme asked. Gene shook his head. "He cut some poor Aleut's face—"

"You know that guy?" Shari asked.

"Wish I didn't. They shipped him home, but the union shipped him right back again."

Gene suddenly felt nauseated. "Jeez, we go out to have a good time and run into those bastards." He watched Silme crack open his fortune cookie. "What's it say?"

Silme pulled out the slip. "'You are one of the best-looking studs in this room.'"

Shari countered, "Whaat?" but Silme held the paper out of her reach. "Read yours, Gene."

Gene wished he were as clever as Silme and could make something up on the spot. He blurted out, "'Watch out for those you don't trust.'"

Silme tilted his face, twisting his lips. "Nice try," he whispered. Aloud he added, "Can't mean any of us, can it?" Silme shook his head, then grabbed Gene's fortune. "What an actor this guy is," he told the women. "What it really says is—" he adjusted his glasses down on his nose "'—ship me back across the seas forever if I don't get laid tonight!'" As Gene's date whacked his arm across the table and giggled tea out of her mouth, it occurred to him how much he would miss Silme during the long school months ahead.

Seattle
Autumn 1972

Throughout September 1972, Ferdinand Marcos planted a series of bomb blasts all over Manila, which, predictably, he blamed on the Communists. On September 22, the Philippine media announced that a car occupied by Juan Ponce Enrile, Marcos's defense minister, was riddled by bullets. Enrile never informed the press that his own men had gunned an empty vehicle. That night Marcos declared martial law "necessary" as the Philippines' "last line of defense." Without meaning to, Marcos helped unite those who opposed him in his own country with Filipino activists living in the United States. For Silme, Gene, and others like them, being blacklisted by their union linked them to Filipinos living under martial law. The phoney coup intensified the demands of Filipino activists, both in the Philippines and abroad, for political change.

Gene Viernes tried a few months of scholarship wrestling at Yakima Community College, as he had planned. But after the first quarter he transferred to Central Washington University, looking for a better education. Gene had discovered the truth in Silme's joking idea that administrators were anxious to fill minority quotas, although they swore there were none. Gene went to Central, not with a plan, but with a potential he could not fully imagine. And though he wasn't a letter writer, he occasionally phoned Silme. Whenever Silme spoke of the urgency of the times and of his own political activities, Gene wished they might be reunited in the only fight that made sense to him.

Silme's body of friends and acquaintances, his activities in general, grew rapidly. Before he turned twenty, he was keeping an appointment book in his back pocket. While briefing Gene on how to sue the Alaska canneries, he was organizing demonstrations against the construction of the Kingdome, a planned indoor sports arena which, if constructed, would eliminate much of the housing for the

17

aged in the Seattle's International District. Silme was furious. He knew the planners of this multi-million dollar project could never get away with building such a dome in an all-white district.

In order to demonstrate most effectively against the Marcos regime and racism in this country, Filipino activists in the US believed they needed a powerful new organization. Silme's friends agreed he had the potential for national leadership, though he himself lacked confidence that he could operate effectively outside his local arena. When Silme met Bruce Occena, a Berkeley student organizer with advanced political talents, he was relieved that he could defer to another strong leader. Earlier that year in Oakland, Bruce—along with Melinda Paras, a Filipina American who had been forced to leave Manila for demonstrating against Marcos, and Dale Borgeson, an army veteran turned Quaker activist—founded the Katipunan ng Demokratikong (KDP), which, loosely translated, meant the Union of Democratic Filipinos. Within a year, besides the central location in Oakland, there were headquarters in six major US cities. Most of the membership was Filipino American but many Philippine nationals also belonged, taking a tremendous risk because of Marcos's favored status in the United States. The KDP was the first organization of its kind to unite Filipino Americans with Philippine nationals in order to fight martial law and withdraw US support of Ferdinand and Imelda Marcos. The KDP members' ambitions were as radical as the Marcoses' were outrageous, but in Filipino politics, extremism had often been the norm.

Bruce Occena and Silme became acquainted in Los Angeles during a meeting of the Far West Conventions, which had been initiated in Seattle by the Cordova family to insert the interests of Filipinos into the newly emerging Asian student movement. From the late fifties into the seventies, the Cordovas—Filipino Americans and traditional Catholics—had organized Filipino Youth Activities, the largest and most visible Filipino organization in Seattle. With the Far West Conventions the Cordovas attempted to update the FYA, which studiously ignored all but the cultural reality of the Philippines, its cadre teaching traditional dances and ways to improve employment skills. The Conventions drew upon the energy of what its members felt could be the future of young Filipinos and aimed at networking the largest West Coast cities. Their basic argument was that Filipinos weren't getting the attention they needed in the Asian student movement. Members were instructed to "do something Filipino" so that the Chinese and Japanese students did not overpower them.

Bruce and Silme were drawn to each other because they both understood that the Far West Conventions, though a step more progressive than the FYA, still fell short of denouncing Marcos and martial law. "The Conventions," Bruce explained to Silme, "have a lot of heart and not much direction."

Through the Far West Conventions, the KDP learned how to initiate beginners into activism, but felt that its own membership was more sophisticated, more politically inclined. Nor was the KDP part of the counterculture as were the Yippies. Though apparently anarchist, the KDP's model was communist: Maoist for Philippine nationals, Marxist for Filipino Americans. Its primary goal was to expose Marcos's violation of liberty in the Philippines. On the night Marcos declared martial law, he immediately arrested Ninoy Aquino, a popular young senator whom Marcos considered his most dangerous political enemy. He also jailed a number of journalists, professors, and student activists, all of whom were labeled Communists. He closed down newspapers, radio and television stations, imposed censorship on a variety of communications systems, and seized airlines and public utilities.

Although Silme agreed with Bruce about the need for a KDP chapter in Seattle, at first he was reluctant to take on responsibility beyond the rest of his organizational demands. Bruce informed Dale Borgeson of Silme's innate political gifts, stressing how Silme was recognized among a diverse group of West Coast Filipinos and worked equally effectively with progressive student activists. Bruce saw Silme as a great spinner of ideas whose leadership depended upon a streetwise charm that could sway people in the Filipino community not nearly as radical. Bruce sent Dale to Seattle to convince Silme that he had the qualities of a national leader. Later, when Silme was the main KDP organizer in Seattle, he often joked, "That blue-eyed Swede dragged me into the KDP."

The Seattle KDP headquarters were located in an old house on Beacon Hill, a district that included people of average income to the very poor. Standing above the International District, Beacon Hill had long been home to the largest group of middle to lower-middle class Asians in the city. At various times the KDP headquarters doubled as Silme's or Gene's apartment; during the height of the organization's life at least thirty other members bedded down there as well.

Early on, the KDP tried to convince Silme to speak publicly so that he might rise higher than a lieutenant who did all the work but received none of the glory. Silme felt the group's pressure, but rather than strive for power he often took on additional tasks instead.

When he did have to speak, his usual focus was the impending Kingdome. He prepared his words on the hill above Eighth and Jackson, seated on a bench in a cooperative garden that first bloomed in the early 1970s. It was as though neighborhood people had terraced green levels to the sky, yet cars and trucks rammed past only half a block away. The garden was a small urban miracle, like the hoped-for restoration of the Atlas, Bush, and Milwaukee hotels in which elderly people could have decent homes—replacing housing the Kingdome intended to crush. From the garden Silme could see acres of small apartment buildings stretched out below, the same buildings that housed—as far as the developers were concerned—the inconsequential poor, the disenfranchised, the invisible.

❧

During the autumn of the Kingdome demonstrations, Silme's sister, Cindy, came home from California to help. Sometimes it seemed as though she and her brother were twins, though she was two years younger. Once, when teenagers, they sat side by side on cots in the Veterans of Foreign Wars Hall. Their father was an Army veteran and their mother, Ade, was president of the woman's auxiliary of the VFW; she had volunteered her kids to lead the blood drive. Silme was tough but couldn't stand needles. Cindy didn't weigh enough to give blood, so she sat on the bed beside her brother, reading the sports page loud and fast to keep Silme's mind off the needle and the slowly filling blood sack.

For Cindy the seventies were composed of one long commitment to political education. While in Oakland she lived at the KDP headquarters, and in Seattle she was either similarly housed or lived with her mother in Ballard, a predominantly white, middle-class neighborhood jokingly described as having the largest Swedish population outside Stockholm. Her parents had picked the house because it was close to Fort Lawton, Nemesio Sr.'s base, and though Ballard High School had only a few Asian students, the Domingo children rarely experienced prejudice. Silme and Cindy were both popular figures, Silme winning his wrestling letter and Cindy earning a spot on the cheerleaders' squad.

Ade Domingo raised her children on politics, a way of life so natural they did not question it, or her. When they were young, Ade took Cindy, Silme, and Nemesio Jr. to help at VFW Post 6599, whose membership was entirely Filipino. Belonging to Post 6599 was a badge of honor among Filipinos who had been without decent jobs at the beginning of World War II, and both Ade and her husband had held state offices at various times. As the official VFW hostess at SeaTac Airport, she helped servicemen during the war in Vietnam to locate in-transit housing or ground transport to temporary bases. Her children helped raise funds, wash dishes, and clean the hall. She encouraged Nemesio Jr. and Silme to entertain troops in the psychiatric ward at the Veteran's Hospital. As they grew older and earned money in the Alaska canneries, Ade asked them for donations. Silme once told her, "Mom, when I was young, you needed my strength to wash dishes and clean the hall. When I grew older, you got so sophisticated you wanted my money and my blood."

The children learned early the political rhetoric of their people, which was either blazingly left or ferociously right wing; by the time of the reign of Marcos, all Filipino Americans had chosen one or the other. Most of Seattle's Filipino community believed in the Marcoses and loved their Hollywood style, however ugly such a stance seemed to Silme and Cindy.

❀

On the night of the Kingdome demonstration, Cindy met Silme at the door with a hug, then held him at arm's length. His eyes had a sleepless, gelid glow from long hours of struggling to do the kind of work he'd once only studied. Silme drove through the wet streets to the King Street train station with Cindy and Nemesio Jr. Nemesio had moved out of the house during the early years of the Vietnam War and gone to Cuba with the Venceremos Brigade, an organization of young activists and older labor leaders, modeled on the anti-fascist Abraham Lincoln Brigade of the Spanish Civil War. When Nemesio returned he found himself listed as a subversive by the FBI.

His children's politics had been hard on Nemesio Sr. Retired from the army and living on partial disability, yet still a Local 37 officer, their father was unwilling to show his face in the International District because his children had come out visibly against both the US government and the Marcos regime. His children took their politics seriously, yet they cared deeply for their dad. Silme, after shouting leftist rhetoric at night, would act almost apologetic the next day in an attempt to keep the family split from widening.

21

Seeing large crowds of people trotting down the street to the King Street Station made the Domingos happy. Signs were waving everywhere: Dump the Dome! Save Elderly Housing!

Silme, who had marched in his first anti-war demonstration during high school, seemed to come naturally to this kind of activity. He liked this part of his life, the feeling of blood flowing, the streets alive with other Asians who didn't want their neighborhood stomped, and peaceniks who'd rally around any good cause. From longhaired students and university faculty to a few drunks from the alleys, from artists and gays to theater people from Pioneer Square—they all were linked, hundreds of caring people who did not want their culture domed.

Cindy pulled their sign from the trunk of the car and they moved along Jackson with the others. It was a warm September evening and as they marched, Silme felt the lifting of spirits and the growing power of their newfound identity.

Shortly after, Silme, Ron Chew, and David Della spoke from a platform erected by the cannery union. Silme and David had become friends at the university, organizing the Asian student movement on campus. Ron Chew, who also took part in that movement, was the main editorial writer and photographer for the *International Examiner*, a four-page tabloid with a pan-Asian focus that reached beyond the usual assimilationist rhetoric of neighborhood minority papers.

Two speakers from the United Construction Workers Association (UCWA) joined them on the platform. For years Tyree Scott had been fighting contractors and construction unions to make them open their doors to blacks and other minorities. In the early seventies, he and his companion, Michael Woo, a former cannery worker, decided to form their own union and UCWA was now considered a model of progressive organization. Tyree confided to Silme that if the Dome were built, UCWA would push hard to garner jobs for minority workers. That way, "even if we lose, we win," he said. Silme admired Scott's confidence, but advised him to hold that part of his speech until it was certain they'd lost the first battle.

Michael Woo, boundless energy animating his trim body, took a seat beside Silme and slapped his hand. "Great crowd! Talk to me next week, Silme. I got a new plan for suing the canneries."

"I already heard. Are you speaking tonight, Michael?"

"No, get up there and ad lib for me. Listen, my plan is to go back up to Alaska."

"Don't know if I'm ready for that. A few last words," he relented, taking his cue from Tyree Scott, who'd stepped away from the microphone.

"Our cause is strong because you people are strong, collectively!" Silme shouted at the crowd. "We talked to the mayor! He knows we're right! We have the county vote against the first site! It's not like they can just dump on us, pile their concrete anywhere! Let's defend our turf! This land is yours, too!"

Silme

Old and young faces looking up at me my hands are shaking heart pounding hope they can't tell how anxious I feel everyone cheering clapping smiling so much power here together but that little boy with the baseball cap on his father's shoulders what's he yelling 'we want pro ball we want the dome' I looked like that as a child I loved baseball too.

Later in the Four Seas with Cindy, Silme glanced into the etched glass mirror behind the bar but could not see the child, only a man worn down by excitement, flanked by a smiling woman with long, dark hair and several Asian kids from the university pushing up close.

The demonstration had so excited Silme's favorite bartender that his blood pressure soared and he had to go home. The substitute, a man in his late twenties, was amused that they were marching against what he said he opposed but acknowledged might be good for business later on. "I mean," he said, leaning towards Cindy, "I see your point, but you know as well as I do, it's going to be built."

Then he moved off and Silme mimicked, "I mean, you know as well as I do."

"Guys like that think they know what's going on," Cindy said. "But cynics like him are as naive as the innocent ones. More so, because if the Dome gets built, they think they were in on the truth. They miss the whole point. The energy we felt tonight means issues are coming together."

Silme hissed at the man's back. "Political enemy."

Cindy laughed. "I'm not used to you, Silme. Haven't you heard of 'infantile Marxism?'"

"Hey, I use terms like that because a guy like him reaches right for the cash register when you ask for his heart." He held up his bourbon. "But he makes a good drink, and I could bring him around if I tried."

"Come to the convention, instead—it makes more sense."

"I want to do it all! Christ, I'm getting by on four hours sleep a night. What a great time to be alive! But if I go to the convention, I hope we're raising real political issues, not just Filipino 'culture.'"

Cindy told Silme that KDP members planned to attend for the first time. The agenda included workshops on housing, which would enable Far West members to see the KDP's strength. It was only a matter of time before the KDP formed a resolution condemning Marcos. Silme agreed that the convention leadership would recognize what was obvious. "We're the progressives," Cindy stated. "They know who we are."

Though the KDP was new to them, Silme and Cindy believed it to be an ideal vessel into which all progressives in the Filipino movement would eventually fit. Then the organization would welcome whites as well as all Asians, nationalism yielding to the need for unity. Chapters throughout the country would connect issues in the Philippines with more remote actions in the US. Like any good organizer, Silme wanted to make those connections: the push against the Kingdome was linked with staying in the cannery workers' union; smashing the patriarchy across the Pacific Ocean was connected to supporting pineapple plantation workers in Hawaii. "Probably have to go back to Alaska, too," he confided. "Michael's got some scheme going."

Cindy shook her head. "Aren't you still planning to go to graduate school?"

"I'm putting it off for at least another year, until I'm sure a Political Science track will include courses in Filipino Studies. Then I'll be a teaching assistant and you can sign up for my class," he teased.

When they left the Four Seas Silme drove his Monte Carlo so fast Cindy's head flew back. "Where'd you get this thing?" she asked.

"Pimp car, you like it?"

"Slow down so I can give you an answer."

It was good to be with his sister again. Two nights earlier Shari Woo had broken up with him. He wanted to tell Cindy, but was afraid she'd take Shari's side.

The night was rich but frightening, loneliness blooming in the

24

dark. They headed toward Green Lake, past Woodland Park, the odor of the savannas in the zoo bringing back memories of his first trip to the Philippines with his dad. They parked and crossed the lakeside running track. A jogger padded past them, her Nikes huffing. A bicycle cut under the willows. The lake lay quiet under the black sky.

Cindy asked, "Remember when you wanted me to jog with you? You said, 'It's only two miles, it'll be good for you and make you quit smoking.'"

"You never did jog."

"Neither did you."

"I'm always in shape." He popped out his forearm but she didn't laugh.

"What's happening with you, Silme? Why so tense?"

"Too much being alone in a crowd."

She hit him softly on the arm. "Feeling sorry for ourselves?"

"Maybe."

"Did you and Shari—?" But she saw by his face that they had. "I'm really sorry. What happened?"

"If I walk round this lake until the sun comes up, I might figure out what went wrong. I been hurting all day. The demo helped. I don't mind talking—I wanted you to ask."

"Rumor has it you asked her to marry you. Don't look that way, the family's small. What are you doing for yourself, besides sleeping less?"

"Thank god for the KDP, we discuss it."

"You take time for the personal, that's interesting." She laughed, not mockingly. "We don't in the Oakland chapter."

"We say things like, 'Was Silme too much of a chauve—?'"

"—no kidding."

"'Does Shari give you enough space when you play poker all night?'"

"You can't be serious!"

"Hey, kid, it helps."

She poked his chest. "Most of the personal stuff doesn't even count against what we're asked to do. I've given up—it doesn't matter, not when you're hurting like you are."

"Damn," he said, opening up, "we had so much going for us! My first Asian woman! Don't laugh. Shari and I learned a lot down in that district. Every week they have these Kokosai Fridays, old Samurai movies, clan movies, real hard core. We'd learn about ourselves. I can cook anything now—crab, stir fry. We were good for each other! But she says I take too much time for organizing, too little for her. And 'marriage is not the solution.'"

"I hate to say this but she's right."

He smiled ruefully. "Probably. The question I never asked her: can you separate any part of your life from the political?"

"That's an easy out."

"I could use an out. Maybe traveling to Alaska with Michael is the right move, frightening as it is. Christ, there's no law at those canneries but the owners, one of their people could take me off in a plane, land ... shoot my ass ... I'm history."

She took his hand for a moment, then let it go. "Don't make me see things like that."

"You, what do you want?" he asked, trying to soften their talk.

"Same thing you do, but at a different pace. To me the personal stuff jumps right to housing and medical care for the aging. I can't separate myself from them. And I like what the KDP is doing, right down to a West Coast, then a nationwide condemnation of Marcos."

Silme jogged a few paces to show her he could still move. Cindy ran next to him, looking like a kid, her arms pumping up and down. "It's just step-by-step work until we get to him," he huffed.

"We will get to him!" Cindy said this so quietly he had to strain to hear, but he did not ask her to repeat her words. She shook her hair and ran, a wonderful free gait under the stars, one duck quacking from the reeds at the shore. When he caught up to her she was laughing.

"What's funny?" Silme asked.

Cindy grabbed his arm. "Buy me an ice cream. I want a large huckleberry and lime. Sugar cone."

"You're on," he said, and they dashed across the street.

Seattle and Alaska
Spring/Summer 1973

Silme's return trip to Alaska after the blacklisting aimed at forcing New England Fish Company's management into a lawsuit in order to prove their disparate treatment of white and non-white workers. Knowing they needed a larger forum than worker complaints to support the trip, Silme and other progressives created the Alaska Cannery Workers Association. Besides Silme, the founding members of ACWA included Nemesio Jr., Bruce Occena, David Della, Michael Woo, and Gene Viernes.

Once again Silme was happy to see Gene, who had taken spring quarter off from Central to help, since he, too, was still blacklisted. All of these former cannery workers wanted to return to the union, but meantime they planned to show that they had the vision and ability to lead their local. While the older leaders of Local 37 were content with cannery management and happy to dispatch gamblers because the practice made them rich, the rank and file wondered whether ACWA's planned reforms might improve their lives. Running a successful suit against cannery owners would mean that the rank and file would be able to count on ACWA to provide future union officers.

The group found an office at Eighth and Jackson almost underneath the interstate freeway. Plaster walls were bared down to lath in spots, and there was neither heat nor water; but the new ACWA headquarters, though without a bathroom, was within easy reach of the Four Seas.

The lawsuit had its genesis during the summer of 1971, the year Nemesio Jr. was shop steward for New England Fish at Uganik Bay. Silme was a butcher, a high-status job. At union meetings workers complained about wages, safety conditions, and frequent shortages of bread and butter in the mess hall. Minority workers questioned why the whites got all the forklift and machinist jobs; they made up fifty percent of the workforce but had only one percent of the skilled jobs. Nemesio took the workers' complaints to the foreman, who passed them on to the company supervisor. When the company refused to respond, Nemesio and Silme talked to the bosses personally. The company representative called them "rabble rousers."

"Who the hell do you think you are, tinhorn lawyers?" he yelled, and slammed around his office. "This is a workplace, we got a job to do. I got fucking salmon coming in here that's going to rot if you guys spend all your time pissing and moaning about who slimes and who don't. I mean, you always did this work! Your fathers did it and they did a great job! What did they send you to college for, to bite the hand that feeds you? You want the union talking to your old man? I remember your old man, if you two characters don't! Now do you want a job or not?"

"What about these complaints?" Nemesio repeated. It was then that the brothers were blacklisted, though they did not discover this until they'd flown back to Seattle at the end of the season.

They welcomed the blacklisting in one sense: it gave them time to think through their strategy of nailing the whole industry for its poor treatment of Asians and Alaska Natives for over sixty years. The Domingo brothers filed a grievance with the union, knowing that New England Fish, the cannery conglomerate, was working up its version for the union brass, and that Silme and his brother had made it tough for all union workers to function smoothly with the company. But the newly formed ACWA was ready for action, and after filing the grievance, the group petitioned the Equal Employment Opportunity Commission (EEOC) for more effective advice and support.

First they needed fresh facts, to be gathered according to a plan developed by Michael Woo. UCWA, the multiracial construction organization Woo worked for, had volunteered the seed money to start ACWA. Woo's scheme was to disguise himself and Silme as students and travel from cannery to cannery as though compiling facts about the industry for their master's thesis. Since Silme was easily recognized in some Alaska canneries, for him to appear in this new role would require a good act and a great deal of persuading. Michael, whom Silme had first met at the university, was outspoken and smart, and he convinced Silme that no one would recognize him if he cut his hair and talked like an intellectual. Their cover included an introduction from a beginning professor in marine biology on university stationery indicating that they were collecting data for a joint thesis.

Although they tried to keep their mission secret, Michael and Silme overheard gossip in the International District that made them uneasy. Shortly before they left for Anchorage, Chris Mensalvas, a former union leader who had battled deportation during the McCarthy years, told Silme they could get killed going up there. Propping his wooden leg on a chair at the Seas, Chris stirred his drink with a plastic stick. "Yeah," he said quietly, "you be damn careful, knocking around with your clipboard. But your dad must have filled you in on all the shit, right?"

But Nemesio Sr. did not understand why his sons were blacklisted and hadn't discussed the matter with them. Silme's father had a long history in Local 37, but during the sixties he had been in favor of Richard Nixon. Silme and Nemesio Jr.'s stand on the Vietnam War, Marcos, and all other political issues had left huge gaps of misunderstanding. Their mild, silver-haired father, disabled for years, moved around the community in silence when it came to his sons' activities.

Chris asked Silme again, "Don't you know your dad has been around? Really around?" He glanced up the aisle at the whiskey bottles gleaming from the walls. "Bad things happen—he knows how they work."

"Or he could make a good guess," Silme amended.

Chris brought his drink to his mouth with a shaky hand. Pictures Silme had seen of Chris from the fifties, seated at a table in the union hall, did not resemble the wizened man who sat across from him now. "He probably knows as many gangsters as you know professors."

Silme's stomach turned.

"I'm not tryin' to scare you. I don't know if you and Woo really need protection. But you could at least ask around the house for a way it could be done."

"Carry a gun? Jesus, I wouldn't know which end."

The old man grimaced. "No, no. Go up there and get your information, forget I spoke. But you better break the ice with your dad, or he's going to the pineapple field in the sky with some folklore you and your brother could use."

❧

Silme relayed Chris' advice to Michael two days later as their plane banked down into Anchorage. Michael shrugged. "Shit, man, if it wasn't dangerous, it wouldn't be fun."

"Some fun." Silme shook his head and stared out at the rain-soaked tarmac. "Who's this guy Calzan we're supposed to meet?" Silme was referring to a friend of a trusted union member, who had told them that the person they were about to meet was a bona fide member of the Alaska Human Rights Commission.

"You know as much about him as I do." Michael shook his head.

"Should we trust him? I'm wondering."

The rooms they booked in the Avalanche Hotel were anything but classy. Men with bloated bellies and jaundiced eyes roamed the stale-aired lobby, spitting on the plastic potted plants. One sorry fellow moaned outside their room all night long. The elevator rattled upward, its cables straining, and then dropped so fast that a guy vomited all over the wall. Silme and Michael walked the rainy harbor for an hour that morning before attempting to drink their first cup of coffee.

Calzan found them in the hotel cafe. Filipino American, he wore a turtleneck under his sport coat and carried a London Fog trench coat. He reminded them of many men they knew in Seattle's Filipino American community who would follow any political lead to further their own ambitions. But he was not an easy man to read. Calzan was impressed by their credentials and maintained he could get them into any number of canneries. "Isn't it great the way you young guys are making your way through college these days!"

Within an hour they were on a six-seater plane, droning through the drizzle. They landed at Kvichak Bay in the first sun they had seen in days. None of the young workers they met at the Red Salmon cannery, a short bus ride from their landing spot, knew of the fact-finding plan in advance, but they agreed to take part in the survey. Michael and Silme talked to them out of earshot of Mr. Calzan, all the while taping with their Radio Shack recorders. They quickly learned that conditions there were similar to conditions in canneries to the west and south. Michael snapped several photos of the crowded bunks, the mold that swelled books to twice their size, the crusty toilets. Then Silme told Michael, "Hey, take my picture with these guys," and jumped beside the workers.

They visited three canneries in two days, then flew to a Kodiak Island plant owned by NEFCO, the same outfit Silme had worked for in Uganik Bay. Each time they landed, water sprayed up from beneath the pontoons and clouds of seagulls screeched vertically into the air. After introducing them to one of the owners, a man with face like a barracuda and a hook for an arm, Calzan took off with him, leaving Silme and Michael with free access to both mess halls, the loading docks, and canning process at the end of the line.

Several workers who had heard of Michael and Silme from friends in the Seattle union indicated they might be willing to appear as plaintiffs should a lawsuit develop. The two men listened intently and took copious notes. They prodded for information based on what they knew from having worked in these places and discovered that, as of the latest calendar year, there were still segregated mess halls, one for whites, another for Filipinos and Alaska Natives; different menus based on an antiquated notion of food preference; and better food preparation and storage in the white mess. White workers were preferred for skilled jobs while Filipinos and Natives were still considered better at line work. When a minority union worker became proficient at a job on the line, he or she was made to stay with it. Silme and Michael knew they must document these practices, because simply to look at the situation, someone might say, "So what? Things have been done this way—and profitably—for seven decades."

That night Silme lay in his sleeping bag in an alcove room near the Filipino dormitory, writing under a cone of light. *Nature has nothing to do with industry, except to continue dying under the prolonged onslaught which takes life rather than replenishes it.*

"Jesus, don't write that," Michael warned, reading over his shoulder. "'Nature' sounds so wimpy intellectual, Silme. Just write the facts."

"This isn't for the suit. It's for a thesis if I ever do one."

"Okay, but if you have to write that, keep it separate."

"Wouldn't want to offend." Silme stretched. "Where's Calzan been, you think?"

"I haven't seen him since we tied up at the dock. He took off with that one-armed dude." Michael strained in his bag to see down the hall to the supervisor's office.

"Don't you think that's odd?"

"You noticed at the other canneries, he don't exactly hang out with his own kind," Michael said.

"What's he up to?"

"Who knows? Fuck it, go to sleep."

Silme squirmed in his bag. "Maybe we should be up-front with him."

"I'd rather not. I'm so used to living, Silme, it's kind of grown on me. Jeez, don't you ever sleep?"

"Trust me once." They fell silent. Michael snored gently and Silme entered a dream. He was working along an endless line of fish, then pineapples, then the sugar fields he had seen when he and his father traveled to Manila in the late sixties. His dream was interrupted when suddenly a door crashed open and a light beamed down the hall from the super's office. Someone hollered, "You guys get outa bed and get your asses in here! We got some new business."

Silme whispered tensely, "That's Calzan." There was no one else around. Michael cursed, fumbling into his jeans. Silme grabbed the only garment he could find in the dark. When he stumbled into the superintendent's office, under the fluorescent lights he found he was wearing the silk kimono he had purchased at SeaTac Airport as a gift for Shari. All eyes at the table seemed to be focused on him. Silme noticed one particularly malicious pair, those of Ivan Bartell,

31

the boss who had blacklisted him at Uganik Bay. He knew it was all over. Calzan spoke slowly over his glass of whiskey, "Mr. Bartell just flew in here, he says he knows you as ... Silme Domingo?"

Silme pulled the kimono tighter over his stomach.

"Oh, fuck this!" Svenson, the owner, slammed down the bottle he held in his artificial hand. "You fuckers are playing some dumb ass game with us, who the hell you kidding? What's with the camera and questions? I know Ivan, I trust Ivan, and he knows you to be one major league pain in the ass!"

"Just workin' on our thesis," Michael offered. Svenson let go such a stream of profanity that even Calzan brought up his hands, spilling his drink. "Boys, the upshot is, if you don't get your asses out of here on the morning mail plane, you'll be criminally trespassing and Christ knows what might happen to you. This is a tough place, and you're putting yourselves in jeppery."

"Jeopardy," Silme muttered, and they all started yelling at once. Svenson leaped up and screamed, "How stupid do you think we are?"

All during the rest of the night Michael and Silme heard the owners cursing each other for not having the guts to take them out in the bay and toss them into the icy water to drown.

Seattle
Late Autumn 1973

Months after Silme and Michael's abrupt return from Alaska, the Alaska Cannery Workers Association was still putting together the lawsuit, aided by legal help and material gathered by the two men. The final meeting scheduled with the association's lawyers coincided with Nemesio Jr.'s wedding day. The lawsuit was clear in Silme's mind; the wedding was not. Although certain he had control of the day's responsibilities, he didn't remember the wedding until he was heading downtown in his car to meet with the attorneys. "I'm supposed to be at the Filipino Community Club in fifteen minutes to deliver the unity speech!"

Suddenly he was urging the Monte Carlo over the speed limit, rehearsing under his breath. "Their lives coming together like two great streams of Asian identity," Silme whispered to himself as he picked out gaps in the traffic. His brother was marrying a Korean woman, which was the key to Silme's speech. Late the night before at the Four Seas he had written notes on a matchbook cover. The emotion of his words embarrassed him now, but he could not disappoint Nemesio and Curn.

Silme's thoughts veered from the wedding to the impending lawsuit. Political work was aging him. Only twenty-two, his sideburns showed hints of gray and his stomach pushed an inch over his belt. His low draft number—not to mention the anxieties of political work—had helped give him an ulcer. He was always rushing from one meeting to another; today was no different. He hadn't even given himself enough time to change his clothes. But he would hurry to the wedding, deliver the speech, and play brother long enough not to be rude. Then he would run to the union hall to warn the cannery owners to change their practices before meeting with ACWA's lawyers in the Smith Tower Building at three o'clock.

Inside the community hall, Nemesio, looking cheerful and handsome in a blue suit, waved at Silme across the room. Silme was younger than Nemesio Jr. by four years, but lately he had begun to look and feel like the older brother. Nemesio was talking with their brother-in-law, Rich Keefe, who was married to Vangie, their older sister. Silme remembered how family warmth used to fulfill all his needs. The KDP and ACWA now engulfed him, but where was his personal life? He crossed the platform and shook his brother's hand.

"Rich panicked," Nemesio laughed. "I told him he'd have to do the speech if you didn't show."

"Don't worry, this is my scene." Silme smelled a powerful cologne and turned to face Tony Baruso, who was emceeing the event. Tony, whose tidy, muscular build was set off by a cashmere coat and blue-and-gold striped tie, glanced in a patronizing fashion at Silme's hair and clothes.

"Glad you made it, Silme. You'd come late to your own brother's wedding, wouldn't you?" Baruso's teeth flashed. "Just a joke. Saw your dad over there. You better talk to him."

Silme didn't need Tony's recommendation to talk with his own father, and rankled at the older man's familiarity; the man acted as if he were related. Tony Baruso worked for Boeing but had a cannery past and wanted a firmer cannery future. Now secretary-treasurer of Local 37, Baruso hoped someday to be president. He was close to a number of hi que dealers in the ID and on his desk he kept a picture of himself shaking hands with Marcos. His was the middle-generation of Filipino labor leaders, but his passion for weapons linked him tightly with the leadership of the violent, pre-World War II days.

Silme moved to greet his father. "Dad, good to see you. How are you?"

"Looks like a nice group here," his father said quietly. "Maybe you'll be next, huh?" Nemesio Sr. was sixty-four, twenty years older than Silme's mother; he had lied about his age when they married in the Philippines. Silme could picture their wedding photo on the living room shelf, his dad looking young in his army uniform, his mother's determined happiness showing in her smile.

"That's right, Dad." Silme grinned. He wanted to step up to that podium and deliver the speech so he could get downtown. "Brother, you look terrific," he told Nemesio Jr., who'd broken from a group to take Silme by the arm.

"You got all the stuff for our lawyer?" Nemesio spoke in his ear. "I'm going to meet you downtown before Curn and I take off," he added. Silme glanced towards his brother's approaching bride, wondering how she'd take his plan. "Don't worry," Nemesio reassured, "the meeting won't last that long, and Curn's dad got us reservations at a spa we should be able to make by ten tonight." He winked.

"Silme," Curn said, "hi. You look great." Her eyes were shining, reflecting the mother-of-pearl woven through her dark hair. She kissed him on the cheek, and for a split second he smelled Shari in her perfume.

"So when do I start?"

"No time like the present," Nemesio said. "Tony's got things under way. We need your speech, then the priest comes in."

Silme stepped up to the podium, the matchbook tucked in the palm of his hand. "We're gathered here today to witness a ceremony that will bring together two people devoted to the same cause." He smiled around the room at the faces tilted upward. "But in a way, also, it's the blending of two great streams of Asian identity, uniting two great peoples, Filipinos and Koreans, who for generations, because of oppression at home, have become servants to the rest of the world. But we're certain that this particular ceremony is going to bring about a change in that venue, however slight at the start, but growing—" He got through the rest of the speech, through the metaphor about a dam breaking, but his mind was already downtown.

Nemesio smiled at him gratefully, although the priest's eyebrows looked as if they'd have to be surgically raised before he could read the sermon. With a pasted-on smile Tony Baruso shouted, "Thank you, Silme, thank you!" Then bristled up close: "Nice job, Mao-mao. What the fuck was that? This is a wedding, not some goddamn stump."

Silme ignored him. After slapping Nemesio on the back and hugging his new sister-in-law, he whipped off the tie he had found on his back seat and jumped into his car, anxious to find Gene where they had agreed to meet.

❁

Gene and Silme jogged toward the union hall. Red-faced after showering at the YMCA, Gene carried his gym bag. Silme was impressed that Gene could maintain his shape along with his political work. Silme's belly bounced with each stride, but it was so good to have Gene back during his college break, he would be willing to run another block with him. "Nice wedding?" Gene yelled.

"Yeah. But where were you?"

"Had to copy stuff for today, but I tried to call to remind you."

"Thought I'd forget my own brother's wedding?" Silme puffed.

"You'll probably forget your own."

"What makes you think I'll get married?" Silme called out.

"You're the kind who does," Gene said and quickly shifted to the business at hand. "How many affidavits you think we got lined up?" They sprinted across the street through thick traffic.

"Twenty-five, but only about ten will have to testify. Slow down, Gene, let's just walk."

"Okay, so it's in the bag," Gene said. "We go down to the union hall, go through the motions of an agreement, get yelled at by Navarro because we 'ain't in the union' right now, tell him reform's a long time coming, it's the future, real sincere, like it's just killing us to go after the canneries without his approval." A smile cracked his lips. Silme felt privileged to have a friend who thought as craftily as Gene.

"We don't mention the fact that there might be another suit against Wards Cove," Silme said. "Don't tell him New England Fish is just a start."

"I wish I could reach the leadership just the other side of Navarro," Gene said. "You should read the library material I borrowed from your brother. It's right to the point. Twelve hundred workers headed out of here for Alaska in 1946 on the Santa Cruz. Crowded, stinking conditions below deck, shit pots for heads, these were guys just back from World War II—"

"This land is your land, this land is my land," Silme sang, amazed at Gene's instinct for history.

"Yeah, from the New York island, and all that good bullshit. By the time they got back to Seattle, they had themselves some resolutions and three or four strong leaders. Chris Mensalvas, yes, our old buddy," Gene said when Silme nodded at the name. "And Lagunilla, he was a reformer. Got shot—no, got shot at."

Silme added, "Sometimes close is plenty. Let's get them legally. We've got to work out what we want in terms that will make sense to a judge."

"Think Baruso will be down here? Nah, he's still at Nemesio's wedding. He's gonna sniff around this lawsuit to see what he thinks of it. But ACWA's bringing it, so it's not strictly union. Give Baruso and Navarro a chance to call us dual-unionists."

They turned down Second Avenue. A number of familiar cars were parked close to the union hall and a crowd stood near the entrance.

"All right, Gene! Silme!" someone yelled. "You get back into the union? No? We need you!" Workers in denim jackets who'd been lounging against the building raised their fists as the two men maneuvered through the crowd.

Terri Mast was getting out of her car and walking towards them. She had worked the canneries in Alaska and, having traveled to the Phillipines the year before and fallen in love with the country, was devoted to Filipino workers. One of the few white people in the KDP, Terri was actively working to link its aims to the union. Gene had been staying with her, strictly as a friend, and recently had introduced her to Silme.

"Hey, Silme," she called. "Hi, Gene." Light brown hair hung to the middle of her back. She stepped in beside them, her body moving against Silme's as they entered the hall. Cigarette butts were ground into the splintered floor, crushed soda pop cans surrounded the overflowing garbage pail. Navarro sat on the other side of his glass office door, the fingers of one hand pushing stubble, the other holding a phone.

Silme laughed. "I bet he's talking to Baruso, listening to him quote my unity speech over the phone."

The smoky ceiling of the hall hung over them like a canopy of history. Fifty thousand hirings had been dispatched from this hall, going back to the 1920s and 1930s. On this spot Mensalvas, Lagunilla and the rest of the post-World War II gang had put together the first radical slate at the inception of Local 37. It was here in 1950 that the union refused membership in both the American Federation of Labor and the Congress of Industrial Organizations because both groups insisted new members sign an anti-communist pledge. Instead they joined the International Longshoremen's and Warehousemen's Union, which had no such requirement.

Navarro stepped out of the president's office and slid up the side wall to the front of the room. He was a short man and the podium on the meeting table hid his barrel chest. He forced a smile. One of his cronies from the gang stepped up to speak with him, then moved smoothly to the north exit.

"Gene," Navarro called out, "Silme, what do you say? You kind of caught me off guard here."

"We just think this is an excellent time to bring forward this lawsuit," Gene said, trying to sound sincere.

"Well, whatever you people are up to," Navarro told them. "I'm not someone you can't talk to. Friends is friends, right? But you better goddamn fill me in on what's going on before I make a fool out of myself in front of the company."

"For sure," Silme said, standing across the table from him.

"Besides, don't think us old guys are just gonna roll over. We ain't dead yet."

"No, just fossilized," Silme muttered to Gene, who made a warning face.

"What's that?"

"Hey, you're president, I respect that," Silme reassured him, but he and Gene looked at each other as if they were having the same thought: this guy was once a radical?

Navarro came around the table to dig his thick hand into Silme's shoulder. "You focking-ay, I got the juice." He cranked his head to the outer door. "Oh, Jesus, here's your goddamn brother. Where'd he get them clothes? He comes straight from a wedding to this dump—he got no respect."

Nemesio waved at the people who were banging and scraping chairs closer to the podium, looking for a confrontation with Navarro. ACWA had so much clout now within the rank and file committee that Nemesio, Silme, and Gene had little trouble convincing the rest of the union that filing a lawsuit was the right procedure, and the timing excellent.

❅

37

The conference room at the New England Fish Company facility, a short walk from the union hiring hall, was packed with people. Navarro started speaking as a mediator rather than a supporter of the ACWA. Between expletives he pleaded for the association members as though they were delinquent, misunderstood children. "Goddammit, these are good boys," he said. NEFCO officials knew this performance as vintage Navarro; they were fed up with him, too.

Then Nemesio Jr. stood. As he described discrimination in the canneries, his voice grew louder, and he, too, began to curse. He wanted everyone to know that he and Gene and Silme were part of a new association with rank and file support, and that they wanted a forum. ACWA members did not know if the company reps suspected that the lawsuit was well along. But as Nemesio spoke, asking NEFCO to make voluntary improvements so as not to force ACWA to escalate to the legal level, Silme and Gene recognized determined leadership standing before them. Perhaps it was the blue suit and bright tie, or Nemesio's willingness to take time from his own honeymoon. Whatever the reason, he was very persuasive, convincing Silme and Gene that behind every good plan is a vital human voice. He failed to persuade NEFCO officials, however; they sneered derisively at his words. Nemesio's performance also pitted Navarro solidly against these young men. From that point on, Navarro viewed ACWA as a threatening force, one that would split what he and NEFCO agreed was "already a damn good union."

As they left the building, Silme ordered Nemesio to get on with his honeymoon. He and Gene arrived only fifteen minutes late at Mike Fox's office in the Smith Tower. Once Seattle's tallest building, the Smith Tower was now dwarfed by burnished glass financial giants.

"What's a 'fifty percent affirmative action' requirement?" Gene asked.

Michael Woo replied, "That's the heart of the suit, fifty percent affirmative action requirement on skilled positions. We got about what now?"

Silme read from the print-out. "Only seven percent Asians and Native Alaskans in skilled positions. Yet we're fifty percent of the workforce."

Gene gazed out the windows overlooking Elliott Bay and the new snow on the peaks of the Olympic Range. "Farm boy needs an explanation. We're including every condition, right? The food discrimination, the bunk setup, the segregation of women, worktables set at our dads' height so the folks in our generation break our backs. If we don't say enough, that'll make it harder to win."

"You've got a good chance," their lawyer said, hanging up his phone. "Federal court. Class action. You fellows've been doing good follow-up, intercepting these cannery kids when they come back through Seattle on their way home. We've got plaintiffs. Tell them our plan, Michael."

"The plan is to use discrimination laws available to us right now. Title 7 of the 1964 Civil Rights Act—some of the laws in that US Code go back to 1864 and 1866, old Reconstruction laws from the Civil War." He grinned.

Fox said, "After the Civil War there were a number of acts passed and tacked on, related to Reconstruction laws, and since then they've been used as precedent against discrimination. By looking at the old laws you can see the legal basis for our cases."

"And if this works," Michael added, "we can redevelop this case and stop hiring discrimination on local construction sites. Abraham Arditi's going to help Mike. Arditi's a Seattle attorney experienced in labor disputes who just won a suit for asbestos workers against Owens-Corning. You know him, Silme? He worked countless hours with UCWA before agreeing to take your case. He's big—not that you aren't," he said quickly to Fox.

"Oh, Arditi will be the main man," Fox said. "But we'll both be after them head on. And we'll win." He jumped up, gesturing wide with both hands. "Asians are in now, anyway, isn't that what you said, Silme?" The late sun struck the lawyer's reddish-gold hair.

"Joking aside," Silme said, "we've been creating a base for the last few years with the Kingdome and Asian Studies at UW and the takeover on the campus. Everyone knows we're organized, that we've got real beefs. It's not like the past," he said, turning to Michael Woo, "but, man, I love using those old Civil War Reconstruction acts."

Gene glanced at him, remembering their conversation as they ran to the union hall. The memories of radical union leaders that had been shadowing them all day now stretched back to the carpetbagging South and the country's beginnings in slavery.

❦

That night Terri raised the subject of old leaders again by informing Silme that he was cooking shrimp not only for her but for Chris Mensalvas Sr. Terri knew Chris through his son, whom she had traveled with to the Philippines a year earlier. Terri loved the countryside where Chris Jr. had spent his childhood, but broke up with him over his use of drugs and his defense of martial law.

Terri and Silme transported the older Mensalvas—and a bottle of whiskey—from his apartment to Silme's tiny living room. His shortened leg propped on one of Mrs. Domingo's cast-off hassocks, Chris admired the amber glow in his glass. Over the sizzling of Silme's wok the three yelled labor history back and forth like recipes. Chris never denigrated the young leaders as did some of the old guard. He felt as close to Silme and Terri as if they were his own children. Even after Terri had broken off with his son, he felt closer to her because she understood his benighted country better. In Silme, too, he had found a mind like his own. He was impressed by ACWA's impending lawsuit.

"That's the only way to make the bastards sit up and take notice, to get inside them, to go right to the plant—that's it, Silme. It's so goddamn ironic, what we had to put up with just for thinking. That's what the Smith Act was about—it was against the law for aliens to organize with 'subversives.' The Magnuson Screening Act meant government agencies could kick 'Communists' out of unions. All that shit from the fifties. You two listening?"

"Yes!" Terri grabbed a beer, looked into the wok and asked quietly, "Need any help?"

"Just keep his drink fresh."

"That's overtime."

"What I'm saying," Chris called out, "they hung deportation over you like a goddamn sword. Soon our whole union administration— me, Ernie Mangaoang, Ponce Torres, Prudencio, everyone—was threatened with being kicked back to the Philippines. And you think this goddamn martial law is bad—well, of course it stinks—but I'm talking about corruption in the Philippines under that rotten puppet, Roxas, and Magsaysay, the guy the CIA put in. Hell, the whole labor movement was slammed in jail. Everyone from Hernandez, president of the Labor Congress, to Huk guerrillas who softened up the Japanese for the Americans to kill—sentenced to life! Killed in jails! Dead from malnutrition! That was the goddamn freedom we got in 1946, believe it! Buffalo-dung Roxas was a buddy of pig-shit Franco—believe that!"

"Same thing now, man!" Silme yelled, dumping shrimp onto a platter. "Terri, grab that sauce. In that ugly pot there, put it in that yellow bowl. No, no, that other one. Jeez, if you ever move in with me, you better get used to the layout."

Smiling, she stretched above the stove for the bowl. "Is that some kind of half-assed invitation?" Nearly dropping the platter of hot shrimp, Silme toasted her with a mason jar of red wine. Terri raised the only wine glass back to him.

"Man, oh, man, does that smell good!" Chris called out. "Bring that in here."

The moment broken, Terri cleared the coffee table of magazines and dirty cups and Silme dished out three plates of shrimp. The two of them settled onto cushions, while Chris shelled a shrimp with one hand. "I hope these are union," he teased.

"These were the most organized shrimp in Ballard," Silme laughed.

Soon there were only pink hulls on the platter and a warmth in their stomachs. Chris sat back and whacked his mangled leg. "You know how I got this? You know what vigilantes are?" Silme and Terri shook their heads, then nodded. They had hoped to hear this story before Chris either grew incoherent or passed out.

"This was the first time I marched in a union demonstration, mostly against rotten conditions, piss-poor wages. By nightfall those sonsofabitching vigilantes found us out. They chased us from a camp we had near a big asparagus farm in California. Big white guys like football players come on horseback, cutting through our camp, throwing lanterns into our tents and shacks. It sounded like bombs going off. Me and a guy named Spider hit the trail as fast as we could for a produce train just picking up speed—we could barely see it, but we could hear it, heading south out of Stockton. I could feel the horse's breath on my neck, then it tromped on my heel. Right here," he said, pointing to his good leg. "Then I rolled under the train and got my leg cut off." The young people shivered as if they felt the night, the hurt, the terror. "So, I'm glad you're going after them," Chris said quietly. "Go after them from the inside out." Then he grinned. "Now tell me about your trip up there."

"Which one?"

"The last one, after the blacklisting."

Silme clapped his hands together. Safe in his apartment with the lawsuit spreading over the map of Alaska, he could joke. "You should have seen me and Woo. We cut our hair," he sputtered, "to look straight. And then, mousse, man, frigging hair goo." Chris laughed and Terri shook her head. Silme took a sip of his beer, the memory catching up to him.

"We went from plant to plant and met ACWA members, got the

dope on hiring practices in about five plants, discriminatory housing straight from the horse's mouth. But we got too cocky."

"How's that?" Chris' eyes were slits now, his brain soaked with whiskey. Silme and Terri looked at each other as if wondering how to stop the flow of alcohol that had destroyed so many of the older generation, red-baited by the House Un-American Activities Committee or private groups like the Canwell Hearings in Seattle, which aimed at destroying the careers of teachers, professors, and actors for a meeting attended or money sent against "the bomb."

"We kind of got found out."

"I thought you might."

"He's nuts, Chris," Terri tried to joke.

"Who knew they'd figure us out? Get this—the guy who flagged us was part of the Human Rights Commission."

Chris laughed grimly. "If you think that shit is new, you might as well hang it up."

"Anyway," Silme said, "I knew right there how easy it would have been to blow us both away."

"Yeah, I know," Chris agreed.

"What I want to know is, what happened to that kimono?" Terri asked as though serious, then laughed when Silme's face heated up. Even Chris, drunk as he was, could see how much Terri cared for this brash young man and how in love Silme was with her.

Shortly after, Silme and Terri drove Chris home and half-carried him into his apartment. Without words, their affection for the old man permeated their feelings, and each privately noted that his visit had brought them back to Silme's apartment terribly close.

Seattle
1972-1975

By the mid-seventies most of the members of Local 37 realized that Silme and Gene had the vision as well as the tools, from well-prepared speeches to leaflets, to reform their union. Knowing that the union was infamous for corruption, favoritism, contracts that favored management, and poor safety standards did not mean that the average member knew how to effect change. Silme and Gene's courage and clarity of purpose greatly impressed the membership.

The union split between Marcos loyalists and anti-Marcos forces remained firm, but Silme and Gene's making Marcos an issue for the union did not alter their position as the most visible reform-minded young Asians in the International District.

A primary question still remained: how to get Gene, Silme and the rest of ACWA back into the union. The need to return was foremost in everyone's plans. One day Nemesio Jr. suggested, "Why don't we just ask?" The other members put down their cups of coffee and stared.

"What?" Gene's voice rose in skepticism.

"For over a year we've been wondering how to get back into the union," Nemesio went on. "We've all been trying to figure legal ways. I got a novel idea—just go down there and ask."

Nemesio followed through, paying a visit to Tony Baruso, now president of Local 37 since Gene Navarro's death. When Nemesio told Baruso he wanted to go back to Alaska, Baruso laughed. "If you can find a foreman who'll hire you, I'll be glad to dispatch." Then he laughed again.

Nemesio went to his father. He placed his cup on the dining room table and chose his words with care. "Dad, I'd like to go to work in the canneries but I have to find someone who's willing to let me go up." For years Nemesio Sr., solidly pro-Marcos, had been unable to show his face in the International District because of his children's radicalism. Now his son was taking a big chance by crossing the demilitarized zone.

Nemesio Sr. looked at his son for a moment, then reached his finger to his brow in a tiny salute. Picking up the telephone, he contacted an old friend, Divine, a "renegade" foreman in Stockton, California. Divine, who ran a gambling operation at the cannery in South Naknek, was the kind of boss Gene and Silme—if they ever regained union clout—wanted to oust. This foreman's scam was so overt that at the end of the season when workers went to collect their checks at the office, some of them received two. One check represented gambling losses, and right at the desk the indebted worker endorsed that check to the foreman.

Familiar with the Domingo brothers' reputation, the man agreed, but reluctantly. "Okay, as long as he doesn't mess around and just goes to work."

After signing Nemesio on, Divine submitted his list to the company and union. Within hours he received a call from the personnel director for South Naknek. "We see this name Domingo here. He can't go up."

The foreman tried to convince him. "This is a young kid, he's just working."

"No, you can't send him up." When word got back to Nemesio Jr. via his father that the South Naknek owner was barring him from working because of his reputation, Nemesio and the other progressive workers saw their chance to use the incident to pressure the company. "If you don't let Nemesio go up," they warned, "you're discriminating because of personal bias, and we'll sue for retaliation." The company gave in.

In the following year Gene and Silme also returned to Alaska, based on Nemesio's return under threat of retaliation. The owners of New England Fish and Wards Cove feared that blocking them might add another complaint to the impending lawsuits.

No one in ACWA had gone to work in Alaska since 1971 as they were all blacklisted. And no one who had filed a lawsuit or had been willing to testify was going up, either. Getting ACWA members back into the union became synonymous, then, with union reform. Now, those who leaned toward reform—on the strength of being reinstated in the union and working once more—had a huge opening and a different goal. Although ACWA members believed the lawsuits would cause some improvements in the canneries, vital human and material changes would occur only when all union workers became activists on the job. Ironically, ACWA's victory had been assured by taking advantage of the compadre system, which dated back to the basis of social organization in the Philippine villages: indebtedness that passed through generations.

The members of ACWA wanted to build a new union within the shell of their parents' struggles, but figured never to become alaskeros again as long as Gene Navarro was so thoroughly in league both with cannery management and gambling interests in the ID. Navarro's demise opened a door. And though Baruso—who was no less corrupt than Navarro but physically and mentally more capable—never dreamed that Nemesio would find the right foreman, it was under his rule that reformists began to take control.

During this period, Gene often occupied the KDP headquarters on Beacon Hill while Terri Mast moved into Silme's tiny apartment behind the Veteran's Administration Hospital five blocks away. Almost daily, Gene jogged uphill from headquarters on 19th and College to his friends' apartment, occasionally rousting Silme, still buried deep in bed covers. Spending nights at the Four Seas surrounded by a band of hangers-on had become a habit for Silme.

Gene was perhaps more disciplined than his friend, less interested in talking politics in bars, which seemed to be Silme's forte. But the two shared much in common, not least their desire to relate to their fathers. When Silme's parents saw how poorly he and Terri lived, his father commented, "Looks like you would've been better off to go career army." Gene felt distanced from his dad, also. At pig roasts and other family gatherings in Wapato, the older "uncles" sat beside the young men but talked about them in the third person rather than directly to them. This wasn't a slight, but simply tradition.

Gene reenacted the scene for Silme, speaking in perfect imitation of Ilocano dialect. "'Is that your boy, Gene, Felix?' Us younger guys don't turn around. I hear my dad light a cigarette.

"'Yes,' my dad says. 'And that's my other boy, Stan.'

'Well, he's gotten to be quite a strong boy.'

"'They're both strong boys, the two of them wrestling. Yes, very strong boys. And that's Andy Pascua, and John. They wrestle, too.'"

As Gene talked, Silme toweled off his head in the kitchen sink. Gene's farm stories offered him greater hangover relief than medicine.

"You got to admire their loyalty, though," Gene went on. "I wonder if our generation will ever be as close. Our dads lived through much more shit than we will, but I miss talking with Felix about ... girls, for instance. You talk, though, with your old man?"

"Yeah, he likes Terri," Silme admitted. "He told me once, very quietly. And we were close in the Philippines when he showed me places he lived. Another thing that unites us is guys like Baruso. He talks about Dad like he let their side down. Thinks he's not as loyal as he used to be. Then he says, 'No, it couldn't be ... your mother? Don't the old guy keep a lid on her? She on the kids' side now?' I mean, she helps me write speeches and comes to some rallies, but she's really conflicted with the old man."

"Tell Baruso to fuck off," Gene suggested, searching in a cabinet.

Silme peered out from a fold in the towel. "Guy packs a gun, don't forget."

"Fuck him. Don't you have any instant?"

"Jesus Christ, Gene, I'll grind you some good stuff."

"You're like my mom, Betty," Gene said, "waiting on me. She felt obliged to buy me all this linen and towels for my dorm room, freaked when I gave it away when I left. You going to stand there with that grinder or make it work?"

"Yeah, slow down." Silme pressed the grinder lid and winced as though the noise were drilling his skull. The odor of fresh coffee beans filled the kitchen. "My mom came to the Filipino Hall one night, here's this banner spread across the outside entrance: Domingo Family Communists! Mom almost died."

"Families, Silme, I don't know. Sometimes I think I got a real advantage over you, being alone. Other times I'm envious."

"Of Terri?"

"Her, and the closeness. I'm close to my brothers, Stan and Steve, and I got a half-sister and half-brother, too. Glen, the oldest, lives on an island. He's an artist, I should take you to meet him. But, you know, the deeper you and me get into union politics, the tougher it's going to be on them—" He swallowed down the rest of his sentence.

Silme shook his head and leaned against the counter, his secondhand coffee maker shuddering into action. "You bringing up hard truths so early in the morning?"

"It's two o'clock, man. But I've been reading the history of Local 37, and if you want hard truths, compared to the fifties, the seventies are a bath. Do you know Virgil Duyugan and Aurelio Simon?"

"I think so."

"No, you don't," Gene said. "They were the first president and secretary of our union, 1937. Got invited out to dinner one night by a nephew of the biggest labor contractor on the West Coast. Gunned down right at the table."

"Man, can't you save that til I've had my coffee? I think I knew that story, anyway. Goes a little beyond redbaiting."

"You, me and Terri were in the same restaurant two nights ago," Gene said. "I didn't say anything, but I had a vision of their blood spreading over that clean white tablecloth."

Silme raised his arms in surrender. "Did you come here to make me laugh or cry?" He grabbed the coffee pot and filled a cup for himself. "Get your own cup, buddy."

Gene picked another cup from the dish rack, tossing it in the air and turning to catch it backhanded at his hip. "I said to myself, those people were severe. I see old pictures of guys like Trini Rojo—an officer in the union, then a board member at Stanford—and I say to myself, 'They had brains like me and Silme,' not that yours are going to last, the amount you been drinking."

"Hey," Silme protested, "stories are fine, lectures are out!"

Gene laughed. "I'm just going through an identity crisis. There had to be heroes of the Philippine Resistance when the Yanks first went in and started killing. Here's a 1902 quote for you, Silme, a letter from an Oregon National Guardsman serving in the Philippines to his folks: 'We went nigger hunting yesterday. A little like a rabbit shoot, but not as cold.'"

Silme did not speak. He sipped his coffee, arms crossed on his chest. Fortified now by the strong brew, he listened intently.

"Nothing's new. The US military warmed up in our dads' country, burning peasant villages, killing kids and women, only sixty years ago. Preparation for what they did in Nam."

"You know what I think about at night?" Silme responded, knowing that once Gene launched into this kind of talk, he would not lighten until his heat cooled. "I wake up imagining bodies like mine, hands like mine, cheekbones like mine." He touched his face. "A brain cavity like mine in the Huk guerillas. They fought Japanese occupation during World War II for three years, then were jailed by Magsaysay, brought in by the CIA which somehow turned the Huks into 'Commies.' They were the ones who had it really tough—but in the 1950s the Immigration and Naturalization Service was still playing hardball. Nobody is talking about deporting us, or invoking the Smith Act. At least not on you and me and Nemesio."

"Well, how in the hell could they, buddy? You and I were born here."

"Yeah, there is that difference, but how do we know it's the only difference? Now, they call us 'troublemakers' and blacklist us."

"The difference? We're making the difference," Gene pointed out. "We're suing the bastards, getting them through legal action. Silme, what's the matter? You're edgy today—what's really on your mind?" Gene tentatively sipped his coffee, as though wondering if he should probe further.

"Terri said something just before leaving this morning. 'I'm going to the doctor's office to check, just to be sure.' Why did it take me so long to remember?"

"I look like a shrink?" Gene responded. "One course in Psychology—got a C—and the guy's asking me hard questions. Sounds like your woman needs you. You ready if she's pregnant?"

"What do you mean, 'ready'? She's the one who carries the child. You haven't forgotten that with your bachelor life, have you?"

"Hey, I don't intend to get married, or have kids. Glad you are, though."

Silme pushed against the door frame with both arms like a

diminutive Filipino Samson demolishing the temple. "Listen, Gene," he said, voice straining with the effort, "a kid is a godsend. Always. The Domingos are such a 'stable' family— Terri's word. Any kid of ours already has loving grandparents, baby-sitting aunts. It'll be one hell of a good, strong kid who we both had a part in making."

"Hold on," Gene laughed. "Nice speech but you don't have to talk me into it."

Silme jumped to the window, scanning the street, then turned abruptly. "Gene, call Dave Della. He's helping that new cook with his grievance?"

"Got you covered, Silme. I'm out of here," Gene called from the door.

Silme

Got this gnawing in my stomach maybe the thickness of this banana will help peel it back I see the jungle me and Terri with a small child the countryside outside Cebu heat rolling down my shoulders red and green birds beating overhead water buffalo peasant faces people smaller than the Filipinos I grew up with some future happy time no more Marcos perhaps one day our child will live here.

A car door slammed beneath the window. Pushing through the door, Silme skied down the stairs on his heels.

"Hi," Terri said, surprised by his appearance. Her hand touched the car door, not yet locking it. "Come for a ride?"

They sped across the Aurora Bridge, curving right and then down to Fremont, where another set of green girders bridged the water to the Government Locks, a place they both knew from dozens of childhood visits. They parked the car and walked over to the locks where they watched as ships moved in and the massive lock emptied. A fifty-foot sailboat lay fender to fender with a fourteen-foot Metalcraft powered by an outboard, the two owners grabbing the moment to exchange weather news. Terri turned to Silme, the wind lifting the long hair off her shoulder like a gull in flight. She smiled. "What are you thinking about?"

"What do you think?"

They watched in silence as the lock filled, a great spill of sea rising up the zippered opening of the gates. "Then I'll tell you what I'm thinking," she gave in.

"Fine with me."

"The water breaking."

"Say again?" They stood near the huge gap of the opening lock.

"Water breaking!" she shouted and a couple beside them glanced their way.

"Oh, that!" he said. Then, finding his cue, "All right!" He held her close, grinning widely.

"We'll make you happy," she said. Water continued to rush into the inner lock until level with Puget Sound. The outer lock opened, engines boomed out of harmony and the boats moved down the channel, into the open sea.

Ellensburg, Wapato and Seattle
Late 1970s

Gene left Central Washington University at Ellensburg and his history major after four years. He was only a quarter short of graduating, but planned one day to complete his education if he could find funding for a Labor Studies program. Besides, he wanted to put his education to practical use. Skip Ware, a black humanities professor, was particularly instrumental in Gene's discovery of his own intellect. Skip encouraged Gene to research the archives to back up what he seemed to know by instinct. He challenged Gene and Andy to learn the specific meanings of abstractions like "freedom" and "dignity."

"Freedom," he snorted. "Do you think any minority in this country is free?" Andy shrugged; Gene felt equally ignorant. "With the freedom to serve in Vietnam, you are free.

> *Acting as your next friend, they give away your country—*
> *one day ... they sign it over to America*
> *along with you and your great freedom,*
> *with the freedom to be an air base*
> *you are free.*

"You guys should know I'm quoting Nazim Hikmet, a great Turkish poet and Communist who won the World Peace Prize. You

49

two might have a future, if you discover your Filipino identities and keep your brains alive!"

Gene emptied out his gym locker and threw his meager belongings into his truck, planning one more trip home to Wapato before moving permanently to Seattle. The lawsuits were well-launched, and now that he and Silme and their friends were back in the union, they were considering plans to become elected officers. Their first step would be to bring in potential electors from the KDP. Then they aimed to stop gambling in the canneries.

Gene drove to the intersection of I-5 and 87, slid south, then up the rise to Menastash Ridge. Thoughts rolled over him like waves as he crested the ridge in his Luv truck and looked south toward the massive, dry country that always sparked in him the same sensation. I am flying! I'm in an airplane, cresting, rolling, peeling off. Even as this thought came to him, he clicked on his last memory of his father, sweat pouring off his face as he mopped out Andy's father's store.

"Dad, you don't have to work so hard!"

"Who says so?" his father had retorted. Then it seemed no time at all and his brother, Stan, was calling to tell him Felix had died. Gene hadn't gone home right away but went instead to Skip Ware's house. Skip called Andy and the three of them drove to a bar west of Ellensburg, then worked their way back tavern by tavern to the Rancheroo on the edge of town. At two in the morning, Skip crashed down drunk between them, complaining, "I'm not much of a father substitute, Gene."

That was four months ago; the wake had been an international affair of Filipinos, Yakima Indians, and Mexicans from their tiny community all converging on Gene's mother's house. Driving along the ridge now, Gene missed his dad, who had learned to fly and then was denied a license because he was Filipino. Felix was like the rear co-pilot in a World War I movie, separated from Gene by a section of riveted aluminum.

❅

Things were much the same at Gene's mom's. Gene cut through the cigarette smoke in her modular house, the farm they once had leased from the Yakimas now a nearly forgotten memory. His mother refused to listen to his reasons for leaving school. "A kid with brains like yours," she admonished, "still messing with the canneries. You were going to be a coach, I thought?"

"It's okay, Betty, really," he said quietly, pouring himself a glass of beer.

His younger brothers stood as tall as he, and he was thankful there was no talk of working out, meaning, wrestling in the gym. Basketball might be an option, but out in the yard, between his mother's and Stan's trailers, there was business to transact. He was the oldest male at the family picnic table. Beside him sat his older sister, Barbara, her eyes smudged with fatigue. She'd taken on the responsibility of her mother's affairs; Betty's sadness after Felix's death was of great concern to the family.

Gene missed his older half-brother, Glen, who'd been the first in their family to escape Wapato. For two years Glen had studied Northwest Indian carving at the K'san School near Hazleton, British Columbia. Later he became so adept at his art that he was adopted into the Haida tribe. Glen rarely came home to Wapato.

There were so many kids running past the table, Gene sometimes had to ask himself, Whose is that? He had panicked in a dream once: At a party one of his sisters came toward him and as he took her arm to introduce her to a friend, he could not remember her name.

Gene took Stan aside. Only a year younger, Stan's body was trim and athletic, his face tanned. Like Gene, his outer calmness masked the turmoil stirring inside. Am I as good-looking as my brother? Gene wondered. Is my life spinning by so fast, I haven't taken note of my own appearance?

Regarding family business, he and Stan were in agreement. Gene was out of there, and no one objected. Gene didn't need to voice his plans. Stan anticipated, "You go where you have to go, Gene. Barbara and I have hold of things down here." It was almost as if he had said, "You do the union, Gene, we'll do the family." Most of what they felt they couldn't put into words, but they found support in each other's eyes.

After two days in Wapato, Gene headed north again, meeting Skip for coffee and a last word of advice. "So you didn't become a teacher, Gene—not that you couldn't be a good one. You were right to pass on those education courses, they're mindless. But if and when the KDP can fund you, take that labor course."

When Gene described his brother, Glen, Skip raised his brows. "No kidding," he said. "Filipino becomes Haida, that's a novel way to find yourself. Maybe one day you'll discover Friday, Gene. Viernes, get it?" Skip said, pointing at Gene's solar plexus.

51

"Maybe so," Gene said, realizing that by mentioning his half-brother, he was really asking: What should I do with my life?

Skip felt his anxiety. "You've already started moving in your own direction, Gene. Just keep on growing with the union and your political life."

Gene headed out of town, first climbing Snoqualmie Pass, then driving through Seattle in the dead of night. He threw a sleeping bag onto a bed in the KDP headquarters. Settling in Seattle, the days winged past. He and Silme met a knowledgeable young Filipino, Bob Santos, who applied for—and received—federal grants for housing, community drop-in centers and food banks in the International District. A first task for ACWA and other progressive Asian workers was to save the Atlas, Milwaukee, and Bush Hotels, restoring both the dignity of the buildings and the people within them. Here was a goal with clear definition: improving the living conditions of people stuck for years in pathetic, radiator-squeaking rooms. The experience was like doing fieldwork in sociology without the need to write papers and earn grades.

The issue of a room being decent quickly became less important than keeping the room at all when a fire inspector walked into the Milwaukee Hotel and found eighty violations. Silme, Gene, and Bob Santos approached the fire commissioner and asked, "What are the violations and how do we get out of this?"

He answered, "Clear up the violations."

They organized two hundred volunteer workers who cleared away two hundred tons of debris. Since the lawsuits, ACWA had returned favors for the United Construction Workers Association, so they pulled in their chits. Within a week or two, with help from UCWA and the International Brotherhood of Electrical Workers, sixty-five violations were corrected.

Taking shifts, volunteers also worked as human alarms, using the same system that had saved the International Hotel in San Francisco's Chinatown. Silme grabbed the last two daylight hours while Gene was content with the span from 2 to 4 a.m., which gave him the quiet and solitude to convert the labor material he'd been researching into rough-draft articles. The joint efforts of organizers and volunteers alike kept the hotel residents from being thrown into the street while new units were being built for them within a block or two of the old buildings.

Silme and Gene began planning for union reform. Pro-Marcos supporters both in and out of the union maintained loyalty to a gang mentality that harkened back to the high status of gambling in the Philippines and other Asian countries. Gene and Silme could not talk to the entrenched union membership about setting up a reform slate of officers. They had been screamed at in meetings, "Just shut the hell up, what do you know?" and on the rare occasion they looked toward an uncle for help, they found him nodding in agreement with the hecklers. They dared not condemn the conduct of their newest leader, no matter how outrageous. Tony Baruso was both intelligent and brutal; once in the middle of a meeting he threatened to pull a gun to make his point. "Let's have no fucking ideas here! We got a power base. Owners and workers alike understand power, so let's keep the status very quo!"

In order to bide time and stay unified, the younger leaders conducted meetings of their own. Over time the older members began to recognize the reformers as a growing base of power, as educated, dedicated men and women. "This is the future, fellow workers" was the message of all of the reformers' subgatherings. Silme and Gene often met with UCWA leaders, Tyree Scott and Michael Woo, who had successfully organized reform slates and battled discrimination in vital union jobs. UCWA leadership agreed with progressives in Local 37 that the best way to stop cannery gambling would be to dispatch on a straight seniority basis.

❀

In addition to the challenge of union reform work, Gene's involvement in the KDP sharpened his political awareness. Skip Ware's experience of trying to find the right group to form his own black consciousness aided him. Gene told Silme that when Skip earned his doctorate, he felt no need to revise his past for the sake of his new status, or to call himself naive for having joined the Black Panthers for a period in the early sixties.

"That's what this teaching assistant in Political Science calls me," Silme told him. "I'm 'naive' and 'idealistic' for wanting to take ideas into the streets. Someone calls you naive, Gene, they want your soul."

"Someone wants my soul, they can have it," Gene said. "That's for Catholics like you."

"Hey, I'm a Marxist-Catholic!"

"With your gift for words," Gene laughed, "you could probably explain that. But for me it's easier to walk than to describe how it's done."

"It's not that hard to explain—plenty of Marxist-Catholics in the Philippines. Start with Jesus and the money-changers."

"Forget that, I'm talking about writing. It's harder for me to explain labor history than to be part of it."

They left the discussion hanging, confused as they now often were by their changing roles. They were both still doers, but Silme had always been the one with ideas. Now Gene was writing and fomenting ideas of his own. Their lives had become as intertwined as the white and the yolk of the same egg.

And now Silme and Terri had a lively baby girl. Watching Silme snuggle her under his chin, Gene wondered, What am I missing? He often ate with Silme and Terri in their apartment, making election plans and talking about ways to rid the canneries of gambling. Ligaya slept peacefully on her father's lap, his large hand stroking her hair.

Gene

Can't sleep headquarters too damn big and shadowy too many corners in this room feel like something's missing my watch no have that wallet safe too missing what is missing I know what it is don't want to dream about kids again Mom had enough for all Wapato doesn't that let me off think about a past life the jungle golden birds drooping tails monkeys and coconuts and swaying trees.

When these thoughts and dreams of paradise became insistent, Gene planned a visit to his brother, Glen, who lived on tiny Hornby Island in the Canadian Gulf. Glen's home stood among cedars, next to a sweatlodge made from vertical slabs, a whale and porpoise cut into its sides. His carved Haida masks were exquisite; Gene marveled that he was related to one who could bring forth such perfection from his hands.

Glen's fine, tanned features, his slightly thinning black hair, the miniature golden acorn hanging from his ear all suggested to Gene the free life of an artist. Being with him took Gene back to his early years on their farm. He and Glen had the same mother, but Glen and Patty's father was Alex Rabena. The two brothers laughed over memories of dissecting Patty's dolls to determine what made them squeak, then suturing them closed with fishing line. Glen once found a wounded red-tailed hawk which Felix—Rabena was gone by this time—let him raise in the fertilizer shed. Glen rigged a hood out of leather and trained the hawk using methods he read about in falconing books. The hawk learned to fly out and return to Glen's whistle.

One day Felix said, "He's well now. You can't keep a bird like this from flying. Let him go." Gene accompanied Glen, knowing how hard it was for his older brother to buckle to Felix's word. Glen put the caged bird in the back of Felix's truck and drove to a spot on the Ahtatum Ridge that looked southwest past vast openness to Mount Adams and Mount Saint Helens. Gene opened the cage as they stood in the buffeting wind, but Red Hawk wouldn't budge. Reaching in with gloved hands Glen removed the leather hood, held the bird aloft and coaxed its wings. Red Hawk looked at them with a cold, far-seeing eye, then leaned back and lifted, wings feathering down a long slide of air, curving out of their lives. Glen quit being sad when he realized that releasing the hawk was like freeing himself. Years later Gene learned a song about the Philippines and remembered that day with his brother on the Ahtatum Ridge. My beloved country, you are like a bird. You want to fly away, but you are imprisoned in a cage. My country is imprisoned.

Now Gene sat at Glen's place and listened to him talk, however reticently, about his life and work. As impressed as he was by Glen for becoming an artist, Gene suspected his own work was even harder. How had he chosen his fight? Or was he born with it because he was Filipino? Glen looked at him with genuine puzzlement and said, "I don't know that I'm Filipino. Maybe one day I will be."

Gene had wanted to immerse himself in the dark cedars, the crashing blue of the ferry's wake, the jays screaming outside his brother's house. He wanted no task more difficult than picking oysters off the beach, the shells littering Glen's table after their feast. But the weekend became memory and he was confronted once again by an overpowering urban odor he could never quite define, the one he associated with lines of men milling around the union hall just before dispatch time. The city was really his element. No jungle here, no palms, no long-feathered birds, no cedars or brothers except brother-workers, and masks only the kind those workers put on to make it through every day of their lives.

❧

The dispatch line stretched from the doors of Local 37 out into the street; several of the new hirees carrying slips were Tulisan gang members. Ramil, Guloy, Pilay, Alphonso, and Manuel stood on the sidewalk talking to Tony Dictado, their boss at the Golden Dragon. Spotting Gene, Ramil called out, "How's it going, man?"

Gene remembered that Baruso had assured ACWA that men in gangs would not be dispatched. "What's that?" he answered. "How's what going?"

Ramil was a small man with vicious eyes.

"The seniority plan, man. How's it working for you boys?"

"Yeah," the rest chimed in, "how's that plan going down with Baruso?"

Gene moved quickly down the hall to Baruso's office and wrenched open the door. "I thought we agreed on some of those boys out there, Tony."

"What the hell is this, Gene? Nice of you to show up. I thought you was helping, passing out slips to some of these people who don't know where to go next. You have a nice vacation? I heard you was gone." Baruso stood up, the diamond and gold rings that weighted his manicured fingers an incongruous contrast against his dark tweed sport coat. Behind him on the wall his face beamed from a framed photo as he received a piece of paper from the Philippine Consulate. "You threw me off, bouncing in here. Never was much for courtesy."

"Come on, Tony, for Christ's sake. Those fuckers are already out in the street with jobs. I thought it was agreed—"

"Hey, barge into my office, point somewhere and start shouting—"

"I wasn't shouting, and you know who I mean. Ramil, Guloy, Boy Pilay."

"Hey, do I know these guys is anything but good workers? God is my witness, they know the routine. They been in a long time."

"Paid their dues?"

"Check if you want."

"Forget it." Gene started for the door.

Baruso rushed around his desk and grabbed the doorknob. "You forget it, hotshot. What kind of agreement your rank-and-file committee got with us? You guys ain't running things by a long shot. Those guys are good workers, they know the ropes, they—"

"—pay back big bucks, no shit, what else is new?"

"Get the fuck out of here!" Baruso backed away and reached for his phone as Gene slammed the door and stormed down the line of men to the dispatch hall.

Silme grabbed his arm. "Don't tell me," he said, "we know what's going down." The room was thick with smoke and Silme's eyes were red behind his lenses. Silme caught Gene's stare. "These glasses are tinted; I'm not stoned."

"Yeah, you haven't seen a joint in years," Gene tried to joke as Silme led him aside.

"We were up most of the night with Baruso and Nazario," Silme explained, naming the new dispatcher, once a decent man, but now indebted to the gangs. "Me, Terri, Dave Della, the whole collective. We let them know we have hard evidence that those jokers were in deep with the Tulisan and that we wanted to stop them from going up."

"What'd they say?" Gene asked.

Silme lit a cigarette. "Baruso says, 'Are you sure? This is very bad. Maybe we should bring them in, hear their side of the story, you guys are always talking democracy.' It was a fucking joke."

Gene called across the room to one of his father's friends from Wapato, "Hey, how's it going, Uncle? You got a job?"

The man cupped his palm to his ear. Gene waved and shrugged, as if to say, 'If it were up to me you'd be hired.' Aloud he said to Silme, "Wish it was five years from now, and we could step right into what should be our union."

"Let's do it. It's already decided." Silme threw his cigarette to the floor and ground it out with his heel. "You agree, don't you? The KDP leadership feels we should run a full slate. One of us will run for dispatcher or secretary—or both."

"Both of us?"

Silme nodded.

"That scares me," Gene confessed. Silme looked away from him. Neither of them was a hero. Nazario was only thirty-five; he could be around for a long time. But the rank-and-file committee wanted him defeated.

"Man, I'm—" Silme studied his friend's face, waiting, "—flattered," Gene finished.

"All right," Silme said. "Now take me to lunch somewhere they cook like human beings. My gut's been acting odd these days."

In a Japanese restaurant on Third Avenue, Gene coined the phrase that helped give him the self-definition he had been searching for. With a piece of spinach dangling from his chopsticks, he said to Silme, "I think I've fallen in."

Silme eyed him quietly.

"It hasn't happened to you?" Gene asked.

Silme nodded slowly as though making sure he understood his friend's drift. "But I have an ulcer from all this," he said.

Gene knew better than to advise him to take time off, to take care; the thought of Silme relaxing was absurd.

"I've fallen in," Gene repeated, as much to himself as to his friend.

Silme sensed Gene's seriousness. "You mean falling into responsibility? You don't do it on purpose?"

"Yes, and like free fall. I might never find bottom but that's all right. You're the only one I can tell this to who won't think I've lost it. I remember nights with my brothers and sisters breathing all around me, so crowded it was like the darkness was a man out to get me. And out I'd go out through my head, soaring. In my truck, too, I have this sense of flying—escaping, approaching, I don't know—whenever I get to the top of a high hill. But this is new. This is falling in."

"Somebody might say you've gone completely ethnic," Silme tried.

"They'd be close."

❄

At the same time Gene become active in union politics, he began to write a history of Filipino workers in the United States. The documents Nemesio Jr. helped him locate at the University of Washington library dealt directly with the oppression of his father's people and Asians in general. The material focused upon Filipino migration to the United States from 1918 until the 1930s, early efforts to organize cannery workers in Alaska, and rulings against miscegenation on the state and federal levels.

Papers spread over Gene's desk at KDP headquarters, notes filled his pockets. He borrowed matchbooks and scribbled down some new or relevant fact whenever it came to him, and night after night he pounded the keys of a manual typewriter. The more he studied and wrote, the more he realized how the oppression of Filipinos stretched beyond US domination back to the Spanish. Gene pored over archival photos of men no different from his or Silme's father, in flashy striped pants, white scarves, shiny shoes a size too big. His face burned with rage, knowing that they had paid as much as seventy-five dollars to some crooked tailor in league with the cannery owners. New immigrants were held hostage by the contract labor system, which allowed bosses to demand that each potential cannery worker pay a minimum amount to dress himself before being given a job in Alaska. Filipino workers were already being robbed before they reached the shores of this country; the process began in the Philippines. How many Filipinos had taken the word of a Spaniard or North American, tall and large-boned, his reassuring voice saying, "Hey, boy, stick with me. I'll fix you up if you trust me. You want to get out of this swamp? Just sign this. Of course, your X is good."

Gene learned that the whole disaster of Asian workers being used as slaves began as early as the making of the transcontinental railroad. Chinese workers dug roadbeds and dragged railroad ties until they dropped from fatigue. Cannery drudgery, too, had its history. Gene read of a salmon cannery in Maine that failed for ecological reasons as early as 1852. As with logging, the industry moved west to the Sacramento River, and by 1856, one-pound cans of salmon were being produced at the yearly rate of 600,000. The market for canned salmon grew mostly from wars. Millions of cans were sold during the Civil War, and millions more to soldiers who manned machine guns against Filipino guerrillas in the aftermath of the Spanish American war.

After the Civil War canneries were built up and down the Columbia River. By 1877 one existed at Mukilteo, Washington; the remains of a barracks for Chinese coolies still sagged in the rain across the harbor from the Anacortes ferry. Then money pushed northward and canneries sprang up in Alaska, followed by the formation of associations such as the Alaska Packers, which competed brutally with an outfit from the East Coast, New England Fish Company—the same one ACWA was suing. As early as World War I (which provided a huge market for salmon), one packers' association bought up all the surplus cans and rammed other associations out of existence by driving down the price to three cents a can.

How soul-killing is the stench of competition! Gene thought. Almost as putrid as the stomach-tossing odor of rotting fish in the early canneries. Who could work there? Who could stand the toil of sliming and gutting fish? Baking your flesh in front of a retort, cleaning up the slop of fish guts, living in it? And for how little an hour? What a joke: the workers received no hourly wage but toiled under a contract that assured them nothing at the end of the season except a wagered body—the cannery's wager, not the workers'. And then they were sold with their friends and sons and daughters to the next contract laborer. And about the time Filipinos had proved they were the only race ....

"Yes," Gene said aloud, "that's how the owners thought. The only race able to stand up to this kind of punishment, and about the time they prove it, someone invents the Iron Chink, and cuts half of our friends and family out of the labor force."

❖

Gene's typewriter clacked away steadily for weeks. His younger brother, Steve, temporarily staying at KDP headquarters until he could find an apartment, folded his sleeping bag and sought quiet on an upper floor. Gene's schedule did not waver: he worked with the union during the day and wrote at night. One night, however, his writing so agitated him that he slammed out the door, into the rain and down Beacon Avenue in his truck, unsure of his direction.

He stopped at a light. Through his rearview mirror, he watched a woman lean out the driver's side to pluck at her black hair in the side mirror; she seemed enthralled by her own reflection. He pulled away slowly so she had to pass, and recognized Leila, a newly arrived Filipina who had visited KDP headquarters with a friend earlier in the week. She had been quiet, and Gene had been too busy writing to say much more than hello. Now he followed her car to the South China Seas on 15th and Beacon and pulled into the lot next to her. They stood between their cars for a moment.

"Got a light?" she asked. His match illuminated her wide arching forehead, high cheekbones and dark complexion. She studied his smiling face before he shook out the flame. "I know you. You're that guy from that place up the street—"

"—my home away from home," Gene laughed.

Smoke rose gently from her red mouth. "You and all those others." She spoke with a slight accent.

Gene followed her into the bar. "Leila, right?" She nodded. "I'm Gene. You want a drink? They've got good red wine here."

"Oh, all right," she gave in, laughing. She sounded forthright and pleasant. "I just come out because my boyfrien' wants cigarettes."

"What's wrong with him?"

She laughed. "He's passing out, so I got his keys." Again she laughed, now with a glass of wine against her lips. "He's a cop," she added. "Big guy, kinda like you." She poked Gene's arm.

"Where you from?" Gene asked.

Leila raised a thin arm over her shoulder. "Back up there a couple

60

blocks. Live with my uncle and aunt."

"Before."

She looked at him sideways. "That's right, you got to be some kinda Filipino guy to live in that KDP place."

"I could pass," he said ironically.

"I can't 'pass.'" She spoke harshly, tilting her head. "I'm from Manila."

"Brothers, sisters, family back there?"

She glanced away. "I don' know. Some moved out, some died. My brother got killed fighting. I got the hell out." She pointed up the street again. "The cop was at that base you got over there."

"He brought you here?"

"I was sort of married to him for—" she pinched her fingers together "—this long. To get me over here. Now he tells me we can still 'be friends.'" She sniggered.

"Nice guy?"

Leila pushed away her drink and shrugged. "You're a nice guy 'cause you ask me about brothers and sisters. The cop don't ask me nothing." She looked around the room, then laughed, her eyes black. "And when his car's not there—big trouble, ho boy." She moved and their legs touched under the bar. Gene's knee began to hop. He steadied it with his hand.

"What'd your brother do to get killed, fight Marcos?"

She flashed a look toward two men at the end of the bar. "People crazy here," she whispered. "You don't talk that shit in the Philippines."

"What's to be afraid of?" Gene felt uncomfortable under her disbelieving gaze. "I'm sorry, it's just a question."

"I don't know. He's dead, and somebody say, 'fighting.'" She touched his forearm. "You think you're safe here, but if you start messing with him—" her lips silently formed the name Marcos "—then you better look out."

"There're rumors he has agents."

"Like it's not true? Believe it," she said.

"They tag you, tap your phone?"

Leila looked at him appraisingly, as if trusting him at last. "As soon as I get to the San Francisco airport I'm offered a job," she said. "You understand?" Gene raised his eyebrows. She shook her head. "No, not that. A guy comes up and asks would I like to work for this corporation with a Filipino name. 'What do I do, translate?' 'No, something better,' he says. He looks all around, invites me to

61

have a drink. I think he means hooking, too. Turns out it's something else. He keeps saying, 'We need good information here in the States, the truth.' Then I figure he wants help with propaganda and I apologize like mad, say I got to get to Seattle, see my relatives. I take his card. And when I get up, he's hanging onto my arm. I tell him a false name, real warm. And I'm the hell out of there into a cab, shaking. To turn them down not the smartest thing to do, but fuck'm, you know?"

"Who was the guy? The corporation?"

"Hey, I just came out for cigarettes and I already got 'em."

"I'm interested, I guess, because of our union, and the KDP."

"Union? And that political place? Yeah, sure. Got to go, babe, call me." She walked away fast, heels clicking. Gene followed her into the lot.

"Call you what? Call you when?" he asked as she dug into her purse for her keys.

"Here," she said. She handed him a slip with a name on it and kissed him lightly on the lips before leaping into her boyfriend's car and gunning the motor.

Oakland
Summer 1980

Gene's hopes for an intimate relationship with Leila began to wane almost as soon as he started picking her up at her uncle's house, where a picture of Ferdinand and Imelda gleamed from the wall. He brought up the Asian exclusionary laws, which he was writing about, and told her how the United States had annexed the Philippines in order to circumvent employers' objections to hiring Chinese and Japanese workers for degrading jobs. At first no one wanted to block the entry of those workers—commonly referred to as "our little brown brothers"—because they worked harder for possibly less than other, more experienced immigrants. Soon racist employers found allies against Filipino immigration among union organizers: the Seattle Labor Congress fixed laws against hiring people of "Mongolian" extraction, claiming they were prone to anti-Americanism and barbarous family practices.

Leila had arrived in the States with the latest and least

62

complicated emigrations, looking only to find a job. She wanted nothing to do with what Gene saw as a pattern of injustice, an alliance between a Hollywood of corruption here and its mirror of corruption there. He pointed out facts: Did Leila know that prostitution had risen tenfold since the introduction of American military bases in the Philippines? She grew defensive. "So who doesn't know that? Does it make you some kind of hero to know nasty stuff about us? You and me are different people."

It was pleasant for a time, Gene stopping by after work, taking her out for dinner. They walked barefoot on the beach at Alki, the Olympic Mountains reaching up through slate-colored clouds in the distant west. Then Gene got the chance he'd been hoping for: The KDP asked him to attend the Labor School at San Francisco State. The move would provide him with the remaining quarter he needed for a college degree, working with material he had been gathering from the UW library. He called Leila to say good-bye and she told him she might be leaving, too.

"You don't like Seattle?" he asked.

"In this rich country," she said, "if I get sick, I got to pay for it myself! Shoulda gone to Canada in the first place!"

❋

Gene took up residence in the Oakland KDP headquarters on MacArthur Boulevard. Silme's sister, Cindy, was staying there also, taking the summer off from graduate studies. Besides Cindy was another woman, Geline Aliva, who was married to Dale Borgeson. Borgeson, because of his anti-Marcos politics, had been prohibited entry to the Philippines by the Philippine military.

Geline wasn't the only Philippine national to have found her way to the Oakland KDP. Gene enjoyed the company of Rene Cruz, a soft-spoken, witty young man with a trim mustache and goatee. Marcos had threatened Rene with arrest while he was a student, which made Gene aware of how endangered his own life would have been had his father never come to the US. Rene and Geline wrote inflammatory articles for underground newspapers such as the Berkeley-based Katipunan, demonstrated against the Marcos regime, and occasionally spoke on a Bay Area radio station. They were striking examples of the kind of citizens Marcos wanted to force back to the Philippines to silence permanently.

Geline, Rene and Dale brought Gene up to date on Marcos'

activities. At the height of his repression in 1977, in order to impress the world community, Marcos managed to stage the World Peace through Law Conference in Manila. He bought Mercedes automobiles to escort invitees to their hotels, hoping the display of wealth would soften the realities of his government.

Rene told Gene about John Caughlan, a Seattle attorney who had fought deportation of Filipino labor leaders in the fifties. John and Ramsey Clark, Attorney General under President Johnson, were unpersuaded by Marcos's show. They arranged a rally at a small Catholic college to denounce holding the conference in a country ruled by martial law. The college was threatened with the loss of funding, so Caughlan and Clark moved the rally outside. Between five and ten thousand people attended, and police hosed them with water. Their rally triggered an instant media response and leftists who had escaped Marcos's notice urged trade unions into action, which resulted in crippling strikes.

By 1979 there was a recession in the Philippines and Marcos began to panic. He planned his first official trip out of the country, a state visit to the US, landing in Hawaii. Before leaving he jailed all union opposition, all the leaders. Using the broadest cold war terms, he made a frantic statement aimed at "stopping funds that were coming from abroad into Manila, supporting a leftist takeover."

Listening to his friends' stories, Gene reaffirmed his resolve to strike a blow against the Marcos dictatorship. Mornings, he attended classes, then wrote until late afternoon and jogged around Lake Merritt. He spent his evenings in the Oakland bars, listening to Rene's tales of torture, murder and imprisonment, which by 1976 were commonplace in the Philippines. Rene told Gene that someone was monitoring the Oakland KDP's bank accounts. "I took a call in the office from the FBI about a month ago. The guy said, 'You're raising funds for opposing Marcos.' I gave him our standard response: 'Talk to our lawyers.'"

Gene was stunned. "US agents helping Marcos?"

"It doesn't necessarily mean Philippine nationals have to fear deportation. That would be too crazy even for this administration. But Marcos is Reagan's buddy. If Reagan wins, operatives in the two countries are going to get cozy. Marcos's boys point someone out, US agents apply pressure. You watch—things are going to heat up. Marcos knows he's in trouble."

❖

The labor team of KDP was urging Gene to travel to the Philippines, which fueled his own desire for an examination of his heritage. He realized he'd been attracted to Leila as much for her place of origin as for the woman herself. Perhaps her face revealed a landscape Gene longed to see in the original.

In July, Luis Orante, a visitor from Manila, spoke to Gene's class about labor struggles in his country. Gene was aroused by the man's argument that if a union were truly international, its leaders should be willing to improve conditions of workers anywhere in the world, particularly the Philippines.

After class Gene brought Orante to dinner on MacArthur Boulevard. Silme arrived the same evening. Orante's eyes lit up when he saw the fifteen-pound salmon Silme had carted south in his suitcase. With his tie removed and his hand around a beer can, Luis relaxed as well as the rest of these adopted Californians.

He hooked his thumbs inside his red suspenders. "You got to come over, Gene, you got to see what the situation's really like. We can break that devil with the help of people like you and Silme and Ninoy. Ninoy could win right now if we could get him out of Boston."

"If they didn't kill him as soon as he started campaigning," Silme pointed out, hefting the foil-wrapped salmon onto the coals of the barbeque. "Cindy, did you meet Ninoy out east?" he asked, and explained to Orante, "Cindy is studying ethnic studies at Goddard College and KDP is helping her."

"Yes, I met him," Cindy nodded. "He's fascinating, but crazy. He talks about going back even though he said Imelda practically guaranteed they'd kill him if he did."

"That's not crazy," Silme offered.

"She's more afraid of Ninoy than Marcos is," Orante said. "Maybe she's got designs. There've been rumors." Orante told them, "You guys don't realize—you're as important as Ninoy. You live in a country that pretends good union people are bought off or stupid or work in an arena too small to matter. But believe me—Dale, Gene, and Mister Chef Silme, Geline, Rene, Cindy—you people matter to us!"

Silme picked up a beer. "We might matter to you more in a couple of weeks. Gene's got a good chance of winning dispatcher in our local, and I might make it on his coattails. You coming back to Seattle soon, Gene?"

"Wouldn't miss this one," Gene assured him.

Seattle
Autumn 1980

Silme marched triumphantly over the bridge from the International District to Beacon Hill. As he headed down his street, Terri slammed their car door and walked toward him, Ligaya gripping her finger, and raised her arm in a fist. "Sorry I missed you earlier," she whispered. "Way to go, kid."

"Hey, you, too! On the board! The whole slate, just like you predicted."

People were already milling about their apartment: Silme's sister Lynn and Nemesio, Curn, and their two children. Nemesio shook Silme's hand and patted his back. Lynn hugged him and raised up Terri's arm in triumph.

With a red bandanna circling his forehead, Silme sipped from a glass of wine and wielded a cleaver over a chopping block. Lynn made egg rolls, the spitting wok competing with kids laughing in the other room.

Terri yelled, "Hey, Michael Woo!" and then he was beside Silme, smiling broadly. "Man, you people did it. You are gonna have a union as good as ours, anyway."

His mother's voice called from the door, and Silme carried a glass of wine over the heads of the crowd. Ade wore tight pants, more make-up than usual, and had her hair piled on her head. "Good job," she said and kissed his cheek.

His father immediately announced, "I can't stay too long—your mom says she got a ride home, anyhow." Then he hugged Silme. Silme's eyes widened, and his father—surprised at his own rare gesture—stepped back and said, "I'm proud of you."

Silme had just begun to feel happy when a camera pushed in behind Ade, guided by Monty Montoya, who appeared freshly laundered in sharply creased white slacks and a blue blazer.

Silme asked, "Check your camera, Monty?" and watched the man's face fall briefly before revealing the little smile he always used to push his way into their lives. Silme offered, "There's some pop on the table, unless you want some harder stuff."

"You know me," Montoya said, reaching for a bottle of Coke.

"Oh, I wish I did, better," Silme told him, turning to smile at Terri who, noticing his exchange with Monty, had brought him a glass of wine.

"Wouldn't you know he'd be here?" she whispered.

Just then Bob Santos tapped Silme on the shoulder and waltzed him around. An old friend, Bob was in charge of his own corporation for inner-city development. His warm, generous spirit and humor had seen Silme through long hours of countless committee meetings. Recently they had been promised two new apartment complexes for low-income housing in the ID as well as a drop-in center.

"Hey, one more power base, Silme," he said, referring to the fact that progressives had been elected to most of Local 37's offices.

The party lasted into the night, people raising glasses, the younger kids bringing out guitars. Gene steered Silme to the balcony, telling him about his writing and plans for a trip to the Philippines. Silme longed to travel with him but agreed that Gene's going made more sense. Silme had been before, and would go again. Local 37 and the KDP needed him in Seattle to coordinate information Gene might send home.

"Been a long time since we talked in that airport bar," Gene said as they clinked glasses.

"Now you'll be the one dispatching." Silme rolled down his sleeves and lit a cigarette.

"I often thought you were the only one of us," Gene began, "who saw the whole struggle, from Alaska all the way down to winning elections."

"Maybe, but I'm not sure I want to keep on taking crazy risks. Our methods have to evolve."

"Keep up with the times? Silme, you are the times."

Silme lifted his pint bottle but Gene shook his head.

"Chicken," Silme laughed. "Seriously. With organizing especially, we need to look down the tunnel for what could wipe us out—not just to seek light."

A flash lit up Gene's face; Silme cursed. "What was that?" Gene asked.

"Montoya with his camera again. Ever since he came up from San Francisco, he shows up everywhere. Christ, he's insinuated himself into our family, got Mom treating him like another son. Borrows money from her, stays over, upsets my dad."

Gene shook his fist toward Montoya's back. "I'd like to have that guy down in Wapato. Me and Andy would take him for a little interview after dark."

"It's not that easy. You've stayed at our place often enough to know how accommodating my family is."

"No kidding, and I'm forever grateful. Your mom's something else."

"Mom's the greatest, she still prays for me—but she's also vulnerable." Silme frowned. "Montoya came into the Oakland KDP just after he came over from the Philippines; claims his dad's Cultural Attaché in the Bay Area. I called friends down there and they just said he was kind of a drag—Dale thought he was gay. You never met him?" Gene shook his head. "Now he's living here and hanging around the KDP headquarters close to our records. Some people want him out, Mom can't see he's trouble ... now this camera routine—"

"Relax, come back inside, play the host. Later maybe you can talk me into drinking goat spleen with all you heavies. Get me ready for the Philippines."

Returning to the heat and laughter, Silme and Gene approached Montoya. "It'd be great to have copies of those," Silme said casually. "Just give us the roll and we'll have it developed."

Monty pulled the camera away. "Naw, it's simpler if I do it."

❉

For months, Silme and Gene had counted on winning the election. Now that Gene was dispatcher and Silme, secretary-treasurer, it seemed as if they'd been taking a stand against cannery gambling all their lives. Winning felt good. As Gene, Silme, and Terri studied the history of their local, they saw nothing but progressive changes, from the late thirties to the present. Despite almost forty years of setbacks in the form of redbaiting, backbiting, kickbacks, intimidation, and murder, these young activists were still able to contemplate heading the union; that alone meant progress. During their most optimistic moments, they even believed a long tenure possible.

Finally the union was going to take a stand against the gangs, which were expropriating twenty to thirty percent of wages in some canneries. The more notorious canneries had always colluded, saying, in effect, "Don't mess with the system." The new union leadership's plan for the 1981 season was to hire on a straight seniority basis. From that point on, no one from gambling clubs in the ID, where money wasn't so much laundered as funneled, would be able to approach the dispatcher and say, "How about my buddy, Benny, here? He needs a job, man. Hey, I knew your old man, Gene."

Baruso was still president, however, and though he blustered, he was smart. He pretended to support the seniority plan because he was caught in a squeeze play between the young men and women and the older compadres. Although he maintained power in the community, he knew that the majority of young Asians in the union backed the progressives. Reform members of Local 37 encouraged Gene and Silme to stick to their plan, but very few in the Tulisan, or Bandits, a violent Filipino street fraternity, took them seriously. Gang members were waiting for Silme and Gene to chafe their jaws and say, "Hey, just kidding, you guys. What do you think, we'd cut you out? Think we know better than you? No way. You coming to the goat roast at my folks' place this Saturday?"

❊

Shortly after the elections, Nemesio Jr. learned of a local Asian newspaper's dire financial straits and approached the owner, who asked him to make an offer. Nemesio reached into his pocket and pulled out ninety-five cents. The owner told him, "Make it an even dollar and it's yours."

At first Silme was reluctant to take on another responsibility but Nemesio and Gene convinced him of the value of having their own newspaper. The labor history Gene had written in San Francisco appeared as a seven-part series of articles in the *International Examiner*, newly housed across from the Milwaukee Hotel and near the ACWA office.

Gene's articles depicted a history filled with despair. He wrote of Filipino workers who for years were referred to by managers and owners as a "discouraged labor force" because they had no home base from which to operate. Many of the earlier immigrants shared not only rooms but clothes. Silme's father recounted how, when one fellow padded out to seek work, his three roommates stayed in as they had only one pair of shoes among them. Filipinos were "discouraged" because their families were scattered, children and wives left behind in the islands until the men earned enough to bring them over.

While Gene painted this bleak canvas, he also recognized that the comradeship among those ghettoized in Wapato and other produce-growing communities—such as Felix and Andy Pascua's father—provided subsequent generations a powerful model. Perhaps because of improved nutrition, Gene, Andy, and their brothers were broad-shouldered and bigger than their fathers. Unafraid and unwilling to take insults, the younger generation was almost incapable of listening to lies, a quality which showed up in the way they took on management, heads of unions, the street itself. They did not own the street, but they walked as though it did not own them, either.

By Gene's fourth article, he was pointing out what many people hesitated to believe, that Asians dominated unions early on. Farm workers struck in the San Joaquin Valley two decades before Cesar Chavez; alongside Gene's words the *Examiner* printed a picture of a truck jammed with Filipino workers in 1938, carrying inflammatory signs decrying the rich owners. The truck was a rollicking mass, coming right out of the framework of the past, searing the readers' eyes.

And by the 1950s Filipinos controlled Local 7, which later became 37. Then they lived through the ravages of the McCarthy period and the Magnuson Law, known to their union as the "screening act." A worker could be screened out of the union for "Communist tendencies" as the result of an enemy calling the Army, Navy, or Coast Guard and informing on him. Once screened, the worker was still considered good material for US defense forces. Silme and Gene knew many older workers who had put up with government harrassment but had been drafted off the waterfront into a remote military outpost.

Reading the union's history led Silme and Gene to an afternoon in 1936 when an armed man named Besant, a nephew of one of the owners, rushed into the Gyoken Restaurant. Virgil Duyugan, the president of Local 37, sat eating with the secretary, Aurelio Simon. Besant's bullets splattered Virgil's blood all over the white tablecloth but Virgil fired back, killing the young man before dying of his own wounds.

"What do you make of this?" Gene asked Silme, pointing to the incident on a page in his manuscript. They were sitting in a bar two doors down from the old Gyoken.

"I already know about it." Silme signaled the waitress for another beer. "You want to start packing a gun?"

Gene looked up to see if he was serious. "I hate guns. Virgil Duyugan had a permit, though. He'd been threatened a hundred times."

"Guys don't like people like us," Silme said.

"What 'guys?' Shit, man, I'm just taking over as dispatcher after Nazario, he's got connections right up to—" Gene stopped speaking. He felt a cold chill run through him. It was eerie to think about an opponent in the context of old violence. Besides, Nazario had never been that bad; he had merely befriended dangerous people.

"What's wrong?"

"Maybe I'm just paranoid."

"Makes two of us," Silme said. "Anyway, we asked for it and we got it—big time. And they know that next time we run for president, either you or me."

❧

As December roared in, newspapers reported that Imelda Marcos had been given a royal-carpet reception at the White House. KDP friends of Cindy's in Washington, DC, suspected Imelda of pressuring President Reagan into giving Phillipine agents carte blanche to operate against anti-Marcos forces based in the US. Though never granted this specific wish, according to historian Stanley Karnow, Imelda Marcos later bragged to Manila cohorts that she had Al Haig's word that she could expect help from his agents.

❧

Nazario, the dispatcher Gene had ousted, sat beside Silme one night at the Four Seas. Silme's group of followers had just left. He hadn't spoken with Nazario since a night in September, when the man had appeared at their union office, dumbfounded at the amount of paperwork they had amassed for the election. He had spoken with such painful honesty that Silme could not believe he was a spy. "You guys are gonna win," he'd said. "You guys got the energy. You're gonna win because you work so hard."

Now Nazario offered, "Hey, Silme, what's eating you? You seen a ghost?" Silme looked into the man's dark-circled eyes and forced a laugh. He had just seen Benny Guloy stroll past the window between two of the most notorious members of the Tulisan. Silme knew Benny from the drop-in center that he, Gene, and Bob Santos had worked so hard to create. Ten years earlier, Silme had taught basic English to new immigrants like Benny, counseling them on jobs and tutoring them when they finally went to school.

"I'm thinking about Benny Guloy," Silme confided. "He had a union job, went to the canneries, but now he's running with the Tulisan. You probably know that."

"Benny's lost," Nazario said in a low voice. "What do you care about him?" Once a tough opponent, now Nazario's face was gray, his eyes weary with fatigue.

"I hate to see a kid turn into a ghost," Silme said, nodding toward Guloy's back.

"Yeah," Nazario said, "maybe I should tell you about ghosts." Silme glanced at him apprehensively. A month ago Nazario had been beaten so badly his eyes resembled sunsets, and his head, a camel's double hump. Now he sat beside Silme as though he longed for a brotherly connection. "Maybe I should tell you about ghosts," he repeated. "The ghost is me. I envy you, Silme."

"Don't," Silme protested, but Nazario persisted.

"You got a great wife, a great kid. Me, I blew it. Burnt my bridges, ay?" Then, nodding toward the street, "And I wish to Christ I could tell you about those little shits ... and our good buddy, Tony," he added, his eyes moving slowly around the room.

"Go ahead," Silme said, his breath catching. "Which Tony? Dictado? Baruso?"

"One night soon. I got to go." Nazario rose carefully, as if parts of his body hurt to move.

❄

Silme's mother had a friend working at Nordstroms who helped Monty Montoya get a job, but he gave no indication of leaving his position as voluntary treasurer for the KDP. Despite his claim that he'd earned a degree in business, accounts for a couple of fundraisers proved him short by a hundred dollars. Hoping to distance him from their records, the KDP told him they no longer had a need of his skills.

Montoya continued his close association with Ade, which troubled Silme. He could not speak to his mother about matters that did not concern him; he could not judge her, not even when his father showed up at their place to sleep on the couch. Terri tried talking to Montoya, to get him to understand that he was interfering with a family. He laughed.

Silme and Terri were catching a rare moment together, walking through the ID. "What bothers me most is the timing," he complained. "Here comes this guy out of the blue, works his way in via the Oakland chapter. Now he's friends with my mom, denouncing Marcos—we're believing him, even helping him get a leg up. And pretty soon he might piss on us like a dog."

Terri sighed. In front of them, the brick face of the Bush Hotel rose from the pavement, scarred and blackened.

Silme spoke tentatively. "What if we moved in with my folks for a while, so we can talk about this up close?"

Her eyes flashed his way. "Are you kidding?"

"What's so crazy—"

"You said that, not me." They stood in front of a produce stand, wooden boxes filled with bok choy, persimmons, and shiny purple eggplants.

"I can't talk to her about it over the phone ... how much for this?" He paid the vendor, an old Chinese woman with a wrinkled face, and gave an orange to Terri.

"Don't talk to her about it, it's her life. Just tell her that people want him out of the KDP office, but he's still dragging his feet. Tell her why, remind her of the discrepancies."

"She knows."

"Then she ought to see he's dangerous."

"Maybe she doesn't want to. My mom raised me so I could talk to her about everything, stuff that would embarrass most guys. I could always be up front with her, and working with her feels so natural, but this other deal ..."

Terri wiped a bead of juice from her chin. "I'll talk to her, okay? I'd much rather talk than move in. You want some of this?"

Silme looked at the the orange doubtfully. "Maybe not." As they headed down Jackson toward the waterfront, clouds gave way to sun that beamed against the walls of financial buildings downtown.

"I'll never understand this family loyalty thing," she confided. "We didn't have much unity at home, but I sure felt free when I got out on my own. I love my parents, but if I don't see them, what's the big deal?"

"Yeah," he said, keeping in stride. "It's just the damned timing."

"You really think he's an operative?"

"He might be."

"What could he know, really?"

"Names, lists, long-range plans such as Gene's trip to the Philippines. One of the Tulisan guys came up to me the other day and said, 'Heard Gene's going to the Philippines, where'd he get all the money?' We're being watched, whether by Sam Spade or Montoya. The guy's like glue. First we asked him politely to move out of the office—he was footdragging like you wouldn't believe. Then last night, we told him to just get the hell out. He says, 'Why?'

and Della says, 'We don't like you.' Period. And he smiles like he knows something we don't and splits. If he ends up at the folks' place, I'll flip."

"Easy," she warned. Then, "I'm hungry."

"You're not pregnant again, are you?"

"Oh, great! Can't I be hungry without being pregnant? I'm a working girl, remember? I don't hang out drinking and eating greasy Chinese food until one a.m."

"It's never greasy," he said, trying to joke his way out of a familiar conflict. "And you know how much work gets done in bars."

"Stop or I'll lose my appetite before you buy me lunch. Tell me about Gene."

"March," he said, "and that's between you and me. I don't even know if he knows yet. That's how much I trust you."

"I should hope so. Now feed me some greasy Chinese food—I'm hungry and I'm late."

❄

When Silme walked into his mother's kitchen a week later, she met him with a look of despair. "You heard?" she asked. Slowly she untied her apron, her face struggling for expression. "You heard about Nazario?"

"What about him?"

"He's dead," Ade said flatly. She stuck the morning newspaper into his hands. He hadn't seen it yet. No one had called. "Shot. A whole bunch of different guns, a drive-by in front of his house."

"Jeez, Mom." Silme sank into a chair. The picture in the paper showed a smiling young man, not yet thirty-five, at a union picnic. "Why, why?" Tears welled up. He wondered what Nazario had wanted to tell him that night in the bar.

"He must've had some big-time enemies," Ade breathed. "You understand what you're doing?"

Silme had come here to give advice, not seek it. He stood too soon and had to grab at the table. He took a sip of coffee, felt sick. "He didn't do a thing but work for the gangs," he got out.

"He must have done something way out of line," she said. "You better watch it, Silme. This fellow didn't have any politics, now here comes you and Gene." Ade was shaking her head the way she always did before she cried. Silme stood to hold her, comforting but also seeking the safety of her arms. "You don't forget to pray, mister," she said, and for the first time in years he kept quiet when his mother spoke of religion.

That night Gene asked Silme quietly, "What happened to Nazario?"

Silme winced. "Everything."

"Fuck," Gene said. "This is not good."

Silme reached a hand to Gene's shoulder. "He didn't get killed because he was dispatcher—"

"He wasn't dispatcher anymore, I am."

"Nazario was going to tell me something that last night we talked. He owed a lot of money, that's all anybody knows."

❈

Silme and Gene were frightened by Nazario's murder, as well as the possibility that Monty Montoya might be a spy. But they reminded themselves that the KDP maintained an inner core of trust and that leaks could be stopped with diligence and the use of codes. Many KDP members belonged to Local 37, an arena in which nationalist conflict did occasionally spark violence, but they strove to keep union reform separate from anti-Marcos activities. Surely the KDP had more to fear from operatives than mobsters. It was clear that running Gene and Silme on a reform slate closely tied the union's aims with those of the KDP, but would Local 37's leadership pose a threat to Manila?

KDP leadership calculated that even if they won union offices, they ran little risk of being ousted by men like Tony Baruso; he was blind to any influence but his own. "How can you young guys question Marcos," Baruso pointed out, "when he's bringing roads, hospitals, and class to the Philippines?" Baruso and gang leaders alike believed that eventually they could convince union progressives of Marcos's beneficence.

The younger union leaders felt safe as long as their actions were confined to this side of the Pacific, but Gene's forthcoming trip to Manila signaled a second level of reform, tying the revolutionary movement there with the International Longshoremen's and Warehousemen's Union and Local 37 in particular. Gene was going to gather firsthand evidence: Marcos' debasement of labor would be documented and sent home to Seattle, where Terri, Silme, and other Local 37 officers planned to draft an ILWU resolution demanding that the abuse of Philippine workers be stopped.

Because of these plans, KDP members grew increasingly agitated just prior to Gene's leaving. Shortly after Nazario's murder, another event occurred that was equally frightening. The Philippine News, a San Francisco-based Filipino-American newspaper owned by Alex Esclamado, who represented the anti-Communist wing of Marcos opponents in the US, ran a front-page story redbaiting the KDP and Bruce Occena. The article revealed facts concerning Bruce's life and work that he believed could only have been received through a link to the FBI. Was the US government already finding Marcos untenable, fearing the Philippines would become another Vietnam? Was Reagan's administration lending a hand to his anti-Communist opponents?

The KDP was unnerved by the possibility that US and Filipino agents had access to each others' files. Now, every phone call seemed charged with a knowing buzz or click. Members worked codes to cover their movements and meeting times, and assembled in migratory fashion, moving from place to place. Once when Silme received a call at his parents' house, the spy game became all too real. As he raised the receiver, Gene's stressed-filled voiced drowned out his daughter Ligaya's laughter. "It's cloudy and fifty-seven degrees," Gene said tersely, which meant Montoya had surfaced again at headquarters. When Silme returned to the kitchen table, his stomach was churning.

Perhaps Gene was even more vulnerable than Silme, falling into bed alone each night in an empty, drafty building. Silme had a wife and daughter, a gentle child who crawled into his lap and touched the corners of his mouth. "You look sad, I'll make you smile." For years Silme had functioned on only a few hours of sleep, but this tension so exhausted him that at times he forgot he had a child.

Silme

Oh Ligaya behind me appears so suddenly such a small brown beauty her hands warm protective teasing her smile sweet a gentle rebuke I grip her so hard she squirms away but first I sense such pounding what is that pounding perhaps both our hearts beating in unison—

Oakland
Late Winter 1981
The Philippines
Early Spring 1981

Gene received a letter from Luis Orante in the Philippines, forwarded from Oakland, which provided him with addresses in Manila and the names of two union leaders, Crispin Beltran and Felix Olalia, to whom he should write. When Gene arrived in Manila, he would also be given names of contacts in the New People's Army and the Kilusang Mayo Uno (KMU), or May 1st movement. The KMU was a broad coalition of union leaders banned by Marcos, among other reasons, for its stand against the presence of US military bases in the Philippines.

Gene wrote back immediately:

Dear Luis,
I'm happy to have this chance to identify with my brothers and sisters, the lowest-paid body of workers in the world and to learn firsthand about your revolutionary movement. I'm happy, too, that I'll have time to visit my aunts and uncles ... I leave here in March ... There's money in the KDP treasury for my airfare and an additional $2,000 to distribute to friends. I've been preparing myself as a tourist, reading the guidebooks, and I'll soon spend a few more days in Oakland with Rene Cruz and Geline Aliva, working on my itinerary and further contacts.

We will eventually expose Marcos's tyranny over labor by means of a resolution drafted in Seattle, to be proposed at the May meeting of the International Longshoremen in Hawaii. This is the step which will unite all of our work into an open fight with the Marcos dictatorship.

❋

Ade Domingo often worked with Silme and Gene, contacting people in the Filipino community who might be useful to their work in the International District and the union. Before leaving for Oakland, Gene went home with her, where she fed him lumpia, a delicate egg roll, and spoke of her connection to the Philippines.

"Most of my kids have gone home," Ade said, as they sat the

77

table. She was small and intimate, completely at ease with him. "Cindy and my youngest, Lynn, were over there in 1975. They were supposed to stay the month of June, but it was September before they came back. Scared the heck out of me. I was over there around that time—it was really changed. Cebu was worse than I remembered, a slum. Cebu has always been against Marcos so nothing has ever been done to improve that city. Visit Cebu, and then look at the area around the palace in Manila, like a show place. But go into the mountains, too, into the villages. When you see village life it's not so bad, it's beautiful. Maybe you can go to western Mindanao, see how the Muslims live. You watch out what you do over there, and don't forget to see Taal Lake."

Gene was grateful he hadn't run into Montoya at the Domingo house. But later that night, while one of his friends explained how to use codes to write from the Philippines, Montoya showed up at the KDP headquarters, claiming he was looking for missing clothes. Then he apologized that having left his country as a dissident, he could not offer his house as a stopover for Gene in Manila.

"That's all right," Gene said. He'd never considered the idea.

"Who's your contact there?"

"No one you'd know." Gene walked away. He knew it wouldn't take much nosing around to learn Orante's name, which he had mentioned to others in the headquarters. The closer he came to departure time, the more Gene felt Montoya needed to be avoided.

As much for everyone's safety as to prepare for his trip, Gene went to Oakland for a brief stay, where Geline and Rene supplied him with more names and locations for possible meetings with members of the KMU and the New People's Army. Since these people were constantly watched and harrassed by Philippine agents, Geline and Rene advised Gene to use the utmost care regarding these meetings. Despite his US citizenship, he, too, could face arrest or immediate deportation if he acted too friendly with anti-Marcos forces.

Gene took endless notes, then drove back to Seattle. He bought a used Nikon for slides and a fresh notebook for his journal. Once his sojourn in the Philippines was over, he planned to fly to Honolulu and the annual International Longshoremen's and Warehousemen's Convention, where Local 37's resolution would be presented. They hoped to link ILWU's power with workers in the Philippines while still masking their aim of upsetting Marcos and the US foreign policy that kept him in power. The average union member might see the resolution as a direct critique of martial law—which to progressives it was—but in order to get it passed, the highest diplomacy would have to be employed in order to bring disparate groups into temporary agreement.

On Gene's day of departure, a March sun attempted to shine through rain outside the windows of SeaTac International Airport. While some friends hugged him, others pressed scraps of paper with names and addresses into his hand. Montoya was not the only one with a camera; the flashes made Gene gun-shy. As excited as he was, though, he couldn't help noticing a man wearing checked pants, cardigan and string tie, with a briefcase lashed to his wrist. The man's gaze was riveted on Gene and the crowd milling about.

Minutes later, Gene was stuffing his jacket and pack overhead when the man squeezed by in the aisle of the plane. "What a beautiful family you have," he remarked. "Where you off to?"

"Alaska," Gene replied, uncomfortable with the stranger's seemingly innocuous questions.

Later, while Gene was waiting to change planes in Anchorage, the man reappeared, this time with another Caucasian dressed in a suit. On the flight to Manila the second man sat two seats behind Gene. Gene disliked spy movies—intrigue bored him—so he put all suspicions aside, drank a small bottle of wine with the crab dinner and walked back through the smoking section to stand by the lavatory and stretch.

He peered out the window. The blue Pacific lay miles below. Were they flying across Laguna de Bay or over Taal Lake, then Cavite, to land facing Manila? They were still a long way from arrival. The man he had seen in Anchorage, now dressed like a tourist in shorts and shiny orange shirt, appeared next to him. "Interesting country coming up. Warmer than Alaska."

Gene nodded, noting how the man had connected him with those two places. If this is the beginning of a surveillance, he thought, at least it's open.

"Where'll you be staying?" the man asked. His blond hair was matted on one side as if he'd been sleeping. "There're some good hotels here, some with cockroaches big as your thumb."

"Bontoc," Gene said. "My great granddad was a cannibal—want to learn my heritage." He walked back down the aisle to his seat.

Gene awoke with the descent, the deep blue of Taal Lake on the right, and jungle canyons dropping into green-black foliage. Manila Bay came up on the left to the north, a glistening city. Then the plane landed with a bounce and a faint screech.

Each time the blond fellow tried to close the gap, Gene moved away. He grabbed his backpack and headed out of the airport into the heat and a salty odor that hovered just above the tarmac. He saw the man again, now accompanied by two others, another Caucasian and a Filipino; they appeared to be searching for someone. He was to meet Luis Orante at a prearranged address not far from Manila International. In his most recent letter, Orante had advised him to grab a jeepney. One roared forward, chrome roll bars gleaming, a bleeding Jesus painted on the green padded grill and gold fringe hanging in the passenger window. The driver yelled that he needed more people, and Gene said, "Okay, but get them down there," pointing to a line of colorful passenger cars.

They rolled through heat, lines of coconut palms, and blue bay steady on their left. "Cultural Center up ahead." The driver pointed to a massive contemporary monument ramming the sky. "Stop here, anybody? I got a cousin who can guide." A man behind Gene, who had been gabbing about parties and beaches, called out, "Yeah, why not? Let's see what Imelda has done." Passengers gasped as the driver honked through traffic to get to the curb.

"This'll do me, too," Gene said. "What's on the other side of this thing?"

"You don't wan' go there, man. Big-time slum."

Gene told him the address. "Yeah, that's over there. Get back in, I'll swing you behind this dump. For an extra buck, it's worth it."

The driver whirled around the sugar-white Cultural Center and dropped Gene at the head of a street that led into a maze of people and shacks. The stench of dying meat struck Gene's nose. His heart rushed with relief when he saw Orante's taut body leaning against the mud-washed fender of a twenty-year-old Jeep. Orante came halfway across the street, dodging a taxi to grab Gene's backpack. "What you got in here, rocks?"

"Good to see you, Luis. I was on the edge of a freak-out there when that jeepney guy reached for my money."

"They usually don't rip you off unless you got designer jeans," Luis laughed. "Come on, we'll lock your stuff in the front seat. Don't look like that, they know my car in this neighborhood."

As they moved into the swirl of people, Luis asked, "What do you think? You won't forget this, will you? I grew up here."

Gene

Children everywhere running in the street squatting in doorways bellies jutting out pencil-thin limbs looking like tiny wrinkled old people ghetto of tarpaper and cardboard hovels men women and kids all lying on the same stained mattress no door bulging eyes tight-ribbed skin smell of sun and dust urine and feces meat frying all roiled together such a cauldron of sadness palm trees paltry shade and shelter spokes of wood picture of Mary tacked on decaying canvas filth smoke rolling up wall children surround us empty hands imploring one smiles split lip pink flesh of fissured palate scabs of ringworm patchy hair I don't want them to touch me don't want to touch them ashamed of my reaction they look like my nieces and nephews I drop coins into their hands look pleadingly to Luis.

"Had enough?" Luis asked. "Take you to a bar, get a beer and think."

"I can't believe what I'm seeing," Gene said quietly.

They drove past the walled section of the city, heading northwest. Two hours later they entered a village in afternoon heat and bought beer at a grocery store, which they drank leaning against the car. The road offered a view of rolling green hills leading south to the Bataan Peninsula.

"I wanted to give you that other view first," Luis said, "so you would feel the squeeze of this regime. And there are worse places than Pasay. Mount Smokey is a huge dump on the outskirts of Manila. It never stops burning. Thousands of people live there, mostly street kids, begging and fighting over plastic bags they sell for pennies."

"You really grew up in Pasay? How could you?"

"It's gotten a hundred times worse over the last ten years, like all the slums in this country. When I was a kid, my district was more like a barrio. People helped each other. Any neighborhood you see that isn't too bad but heading that way is against Marcos and martial law. When you see peasants, you aren't seeing 'potential leftists' or whatever Washington, DC, calls them, you're seeing the new army itself. No one here is fooled by Marcos, except those who already have power and money, or live on the take."

While Luis drove west through villages towards Subic Bay, Gene was lulled into sleep by the heat and beer. He started awake to a

81

nightmare of bars, women, and sailors, waving at them from the streets. "We passed up the bases at Clark and Angeles," Luis said. "I thought I'd give you a look at this little hell. Want to stop, get a Pepsi? Tattoo? Knifed?"

Crew-cut sailors wove drunkenly down the sidewalks, arms around women whose dress and actions radically contrasted with those Gene had noticed in the places they'd passed through earlier. The village women had appeared demure, their dresses bright but modest, their hair dark and soft under their scarves. Here on the military base Gene saw more beautiful women, but now dressed in blouses that revealed breasts, mini-skirts hiked above thighs, hair gleaming with spray.

Disco music from the bars rumbled up the back of Gene's neck, the bass drowning out Luis's words. The smell of grease and meat from the fast-food joints made Gene aware of his hunger despite the raunchiness.

"This is the outpost of American civilization, Gene," Luis said. "At Clark it's even worse. Guards shoot Filipinos if they go after the scrap metal piled up beside the base. Three golf courses on some of the best farmland in the area. Filipinos connected to American bases make one-tenth the wages of people doing the same work in Japan."

Luis pushed north and west past endless villages. The land became more rural as they entered the province of Pangasinan. Finally, they stopped at what looked like a house but was actually a little fish fry with a thatched palm roof, no sign out front. Gossamer fishnets hung on a line in the yard. The cook yelled a greeting at Luis in Tagalog and Gene was introduced as they flopped into seats next to a grill on hot coals. Drinking beer in the near-dark, Gene realized that the sound outside the open veranda door was the slur of the South China Sea. Within minutes a delicately cooked fish lay before him on a palm leaf. He ate ravenously, following Luis' instructions to fillet and pull out the backbone. They feasted on fish and prawns and something in a shell Gene did not ask about, because it was good and he was afraid he might hear, "In Pangasinan we enjoy sea slugs."

That night Gene and Luis shared a cabana on the sand, their bags spread over benches woven of fronds. "Want to swim?" Luis asked. "It's like a tub, no sharks here. Well, not many. Just don't go out too far. The water's protected in here, you'll see in the morning."

Gene considered wearing his underwear, then realized how sandy it would feel in the morning. Gingerly he entered the water naked.

Totally exposing himself to what he imagined were hungry, darting fish made him nervous, but the first rolling warmth of the surf cleansed his fear. He lay on his back, his friend nearby, and slowly turned in the sea. The incoming tide brought the two men back to shore and they walked heavily up the beach.

Gene slept soundly. Late in the morning he awoke to a chicken pecking at his watch. He shot his arm straight up, and the bird went squawking to the roof of the cabana.

They pushed farther north, heading through Pangasinan to the little town of Tuloan. From the twisting road, green mountains rose to the east and the blue China Sea shimmered to the west. Carabaos pulled wagons heaped high with frond baskets and palm leaves. Young men wearing shorts and straw hats, with long poles across their shoulders, waved and yelled to them in a dialect unfamiliar to Gene's ears.

The jeep cut along the edge of an enormous system of rice paddies, terraced downward, each designed to receive water from the one above, an ancient agricultural technique still in practice. They circled through a valley that widened out into huge plains of grass, tassled silver. In every village they passed, newly harvested mangos glowed in piles in the markets.

It didn't take much asking in the tiny village of Tuloan to find Gene's father's cousins. Luis left quickly, en route to Central Luzon to arrange a meeting with two leaders of the KMU movement. Soon the villagers had seated Gene on a tough little pony, its hairy sides spiking his bare legs, while several wide-eyed youngsters fought cheerfully to carry his backpack and suitcase.

Gene's uncle Leo spoke a little English; otherwise Gene would have been lost. When Leo reached toward his nephew's face, Gene took the old man's wrist, placed his hand against his own forehead, and said, "Lolo, Grandfather." He had memorized phrases from a book on Tagalog, but whenever he opened his mouth to say, "thanks," or "shall we go today or tomorrow," the children fell to the ground laughing. He passed out bubble gum to at least a dozen kids—a few, he was relieved to hear, were not related—and red and blue bubbles suddenly filled the room, snapping, bursting onto faces, into hair. Gene wondered if this were the first time they had ever chewed gum.

Through Uncle Leo, the children learned that Gene used to wrestle. With gleeful shouts and laughter, they grabbed his hands and led him to the grassy yard. Gene stripped off his shirt, and under mango blossoms as big as orchids, he wrestled five or six boys and girls, who, whenever they pinned their big cousin, laughed so hysterically they lost their holds.

Maria, Uncle Leo's wife, was short and lively with a waistline like the circumference of the globe. Gene wondered if she were pregnant again, despite her age and all their children. Maria swept the dirt floor with banana leaves, then fed him a mango and bread she'd baked on a rack on the open fire. The bread reminded Gene of Yakima frybread from back home. Gene had been warned that in every Filipino household he would be treated like a king, given the most tender piece of meat, the most comfortable bed, and that rather than turn them down, he should accept their generosity.

Leo explained that they had plenty of food and that they had planned a pig roast in his honor that night; the whole neighborhood was chipping in. The barrio was situated near several rice fields but no one appeared to be well off materially. When Gene asked Leo about unionizing, Leo seemed not to understand—or unwilling to discuss the issue.

All day villagers passed by their open door, spying Gene, then running off. He fell asleep in a back room, thatched and open to the wind but for a piece of tattered netting. He had tried to ask about the mosquitoes—"the kind that make you need white pills?"—but his uncle had shrugged. Before lying down, Gene rubbed insect repellent into his skin, but some of the mosquitoes looked big enough to penetrate wood.

At sunset he awoke, dizzy and still jet-lagged, but aware that a party was in progress. As he lay there dozing, he dreamed of chasing a wild boar through a jungle of muck, shoes sucking at every step, the trapped boar turning threatening tusks. He shook the dream out of his head and dressed quickly.

In the center of the barrio, sparks flew up through an enormous grill, rising into the palms and the scented night. As soon as they spied Gene, the children cried, "Biyernes! Biyernes!" Several people shook his hand, and one handed him a bottle of San Miguel. He was relieved to hear a couple of men his age speaking English. In the States Gene was of average height, but here he looked down upon a sea of smiling faces. He watched three sucklings, pierced from mouth to anus, slowly turn on the spit, an odd experience for a man who'd recently dreamed of being attacked.

"Can you show me where you work tomorrow?" Gene asked the man who was giving the pigs a turn.

"Tomorrow Sunday, show you church." The man grinned and drifted off, leaving Gene to wonder if he remembered how to cross himself.

Welcoming the solitary moment in the warmth of the evening, Gene looked around the yard. The younger women were small, thin and dark, eyes bright in the half-darkness when they glanced his way and then ducked their heads shyly. One, wearing a flowered dress and a blossom in her hair, led him to Roi, who spoke the best English. Roi told Gene he'd take him to work with him in the pineapple fields on Monday. "Great," Gene agreed. "What's the starting pay?" Several people around him laughed when Roi translated.

"Not too much," Roi answered.

After eating, they sat around the dying fire, the grill now pulled off, laughing and licking fingers, passing glasses of tubak, an alcoholic beverage made from the milk of coconuts.

"You need a union," Gene advised.

This time no one laughed. "What for?" Roi said. "The landowner's in hock up to his obot to the Americans, anyhow."

"Dole? Up to his what?"

Roi patted his behind.

Later, lying on a cot in his sleeping bag under netting improved by additional pieces Maria had gotten from a neighbor, Gene stared at the bright crescent moon. The phrase "discouraged work force" irritated his thoughts like teeth hitting sand in a steamed clam. His family and their neighbors were hospitable and loving, but he had noted that the children's otherwise handsome bodies were not quite filled out. He joked to himself that if he stuck around to organize, first he'd have to talk a number of these devout Catholics into using birth control. But what kept him really awake was the eerie but comforting feeling of coming home to exactly what he'd expected. "I'm falling in," he had told Silme shortly after he'd left the university. Now he was falling deeper. The strangest feeling, however, was that while he was here to learn to become a stronger organizer, this place promised him liberation. In this wet darkness, with birds and long-tailed macque monkeys knocking voices in the nearby woods, Gene felt he could fall a long way from responsibility and not miss it a bit.

❈

85

The next morning, the entire village turned out for church, walking from all directions in the blazing sun toward a tall stucco building that dated to the sixteenth century. Ornate Spanish carvings and terra cotta statues of saints stood against two-feet-thick walls and passageways draped with bougainvillea. Gene, who had expected gaudiness, was stunned by the subdued beauty. He touched the holy water and made the sign of the cross. A choir sang the hymns' choruses a cappella, an almost ethereal sound. Gene was disappointed when the singing stopped. He wished now that Silme and Cindy had invited him along when they occasionally attended church in Seattle. Eyes widened along his row when he dropped a dollar in the plate, but he had nothing smaller. He planned to leave more money with his relatives, anyway.

❋

By mid-Monday afternoon in the pineapple fields, Gene's back felt permanently cramped from bending over sharp leaves, his hand raw from the machete. A child ran toward him, cranking his arm in a circular motion by his ear. "Mr. Biyernes, ding ding ding!" At the end of the row, Gene hopped on a bicycle to ride to the phone at the store. Soon he heard Luis laughing on the other end. "What do you think you're doing? Organizers don't work, they sit on their asses!" He gave Gene an address in Malolos, where Aguinaldo had first gathered his forces to declare an independent Philippines in 1889. By the end of the ensuing war with US troops, 200,000 Filipinos had been killed, and the United States was the new colonial power. Gene made plans to meet Luis there the following afternoon.

"Catch an early bus," Luis advised. "They'll go out of their way to get you if you tell the storekeeper to call the stop ahead."

The next morning, dew still wet on the mango leaves, Gene headed into the village with his uncle, again on the bristle-haired pony, backpack and bag attached. When Gene tried to press five dollars into Leo's hand and was turned down, he was especially glad he had dropped two twenties into his family's sugar bowl before leaving. No doubt they would use the money for the whole barrio. Gene had also left several shirts for the kids and pictures of his family in the States, which his aunt, Maria, had placed on their nightstand.

As the morning heated up, Gene's head knocked sleepily against the bus window. Most of the poultry and goats were gone by the time they reached the outskirts of Malolos. Luis met Gene at a hostel downtown and filled him in on the next day's meeting. They were planning a demonstration against martial law, either in Malolos or farther west in Bulacan, a warm-up to the nationwide demonstrations planned for May 1. Sitting in a small restaurant near the original spot of Aguinaldo's constitutional assembly, they talked about Gene's visit with his relatives and thought beyond their impending meeting.

Luis understood Gene's feeling for village life, the sense of freedom he had experienced in such a short time. "I may be a Manila boy," Luis said, "but in the last few years I've been getting out." He suggested that Gene arrange a mountain trip when he went south to meet members of the New Peoples' Army. "Those young guys you met in the village may well be in the NPA. They wouldn't tell you. You look safe, but they're so used to the CIA nosing around, they're on edge, especially if they have guns."

Gene raised his eyebrows.

"And maybe just before you leave the Philippines," Luis continued, "you should travel on your own, up in the northwest, if you want to lose yourself. You won't forget it."

The next day they met Felix Olalia, president of the KMU, and Crispin Beltran, general secretary. Felix, dressed in jeans, was young and tense; Crispin, the veteran, seemed weary, his face lined with fatigue. They greeted Gene warmly in their hotel room, offering him coffee, fruit, and a delicious muffin-like bread. They told him how the KMU was growing stronger daily and how impressed they were that the ILWU and Local 37 were once again electing progressive officers. Both men had spent time in the US, one of them having worked a season in Alaska in the late sixties. Gene quickly forgot the clandestine nature of their get-together in the face of their simple humanity. Like Gene and Silme, these men were labor organizers, maintaining the same goals, but living an existence that forced them into constant vigilance.

"You talk about the right to collectively bargain, to strike—these things don't exist here. The so-called unions that Marcos allows are merely people in his hire, window dressing. If someone asks him how unions are doing, he pulls these guys out and says, 'Sure, we got good work relations here. See the fat tummy?' But if a real union rep makes a wrong move, he's jailed," Olalia said. He turned to Beltran. "And don't start smoking now, you'll tempt me, I just quit."

"Talk about autocratic," the older man said, pushing a cigarette back into his pack.

The four men pored over material they wanted to include in the resolution to be presented at the International Longshoremen's and Warehousemen's Union Convention in May. Again, Beltran and Olalia were impressed with Local 37's willingness to risk helping them in their fight by linking its name to the May 1st Movement.

"Everybody on the executive committee is against Marcos?" Beltran asked, his voice rising with disbelief.

"I guess we'll find out."

"They'll all be pressured by Marcos's regime. You won't believe how many Marcos supporters are in Hawaii. Diplomats, agents—they're like lice on a dead fish. You'll be pressured, too. Have you been spotted yet?"

Gene told him about the men on his flights and in the airport. They shook their heads. "Maybe, maybe not, you might be lucky," Olalia said. He pulled back the curtain to look into the street.

But when they broke for lunch, no more than two steps through the front entrance, Gene saw the camera aimed at the four of them from the roof across the street. Surrounding the man squatted behind it were two other men in street clothes and one uniformed policeman. They heard the clicks of the shutter before they were able to avert their faces. The camera had a huge close-up lens. "Sorry about that," Luis said, as he hurriedly led them into the back of a Chinese restaurant.

"Baptism of fire for Gene," Beltran said. "We're used to it. But how the hell did they know we were here?"

"Better go to Plan B for tomorrow," Olalia put in.

"They'll be there tomorrow, too, just different faces," Luis said. "Still, we have to go through with it."

An easy bravado ran through their lunch talk, but throughout the day and into the night, Gene kept seeing the spies on the roof. In his room at the hostel, he tossed in his sleeping bag while music reverberated from the transistor earphones of a sailor who had smoked two joints and was now snoring loudly. Gene switched off the man's radio and turned him onto his face.

Still awake, Gene attempted to second-guess the logic of martial law. He was seen with known opposition people, photographed with them. How did any government agency necessarily know his intentions? Simple: passports, recent entries; he probably already appeared on a list, and they had his photo. Perhaps he had already been tagged at home. A US agent enters the passport office, flashes a badge. No. Gene knew he had to forget this paranoia and go to sleep. But he also realized there were ways for agents to know his movements. It was their job, and much higher-paying than his.

❦

It was the beginning of Holy Week, the week of Palm Blessing, and it was hot. It was wonderful how this religious festival of wild, colorful masks and wooden faces that resembled ancient South Sea Islanders hid people with other motives. As soon as the red-and-gold garbed, blaring band turned a corner into a vacant lot in a barrio, everyone began to shout, "Down with Marcos and martial law!" The shouting was serious, but only a companion to the celebration of gleeful children and barking dogs. Then the police broke in trying to arrest people, but had trouble doing so. No guns were fired. The police, knowing that May 1 was coming, may only have been warming themselves up.

❦

Gene stayed two nights with Uncle Manuelo who lived in a Manila suburb. This uncle, educated in the US, spoke English. Now retired, Manuelo used to run a physical education program in the grade schools. Proudly, he toured Gene through the palm-lined, middle-class neighborhood, pausing at a school yard where boys and girls wearing soccer cleats and long socks played a rousing game of basketball on a dirt court. His uncle spoke fondly of his brother, Felix, and Gene was thankful he had written to tell Manuelo of his father's death in 1978. In the morning, Vange, Manuelo's wife, cooked sinigang, a wonderful, lime-flavored soup with fish and vegetables. Gene felt so comfortable he even tried saying a few Tagalog expressions to her.

"Masarap!" he enthused over the fish. "I was very nagugutom!"

He left on a Friday, explaining that he and Luis had only the weekend to climb Mount Apo. "Oh, that's beautiful," they said. "You will love that. But you must come back to see us before you leave the Philippines."

Gene and Luis flew to Davao. Before climbing Mount Apo, they met with Julio, a lawyer from Davao, and a schoolteacher from Cebu. The two men emerged mysteriously from the brush at a road junction, unwilling to risk being seen and possibly photographed with Luis.

Both men, wearing jeans, T shirts and bands of blue silk wrapped tightly around their heads, seemed like Filipino versions of Gene's fellow KDP members—politically exuberant but smaller in stature, their faces more sharply sculpted. The most important struggle for nationalists, including these two members of the New People's Army, was to build the revolution at home. Therefore they were surprised to hear Gene describe the KDP's two-dimensional aims: first, to fight racism everywhere; second, to work for changes in the Philippines. Filipino nationalists believed that fighting racism put too much of a drain on resources. As these young enthusiasts talked, Gene thought of Rene Cruz, who, despite his nationalism, put the fight against racism first. These men believed that eventually all Filipino people would return to the Islands. Intensely loyal to their revolution, they assumed that Gene's first visit to his "native land" was his first step toward returning permanently. Their naive revision of Gene's complex plans heightened his own newly acquired sense of confusion: perhaps he did want to live here.

❧

The higher Gene and Luis climbed, the more striking the views: first the vast, sloping jungle tops, next the bright, distant sea. Climbing steadily, they reached the last assault post and looked up toward the summit, approximately six thousand feet in altitude. Trees tailed off to scrub and volcanic rock that protruded like blackened bones.

Piles of yellow-gold sulfur steamed in craters beneath them. But the air was so fine as they climbed the last few hundred yards that the gaseous odor grew less repugnant. From the hard-bitten top they reveled in 360 degrees of Sulu Sea, Gulf of Mindanao, and Pacific Ocean—in all directions, a blue-green infinity. Below lay Mindanao, so divided between Muslims and Christians that Marcos had given up on the western extreme of the place.

The following night, in a village north of Davao City, Gene recuperated from the hike and met with Julio's NPA associates. During the day this cadre worked on one of the largest turkey farms in the world; at night the members gathered, armed with weapons procured from five other countries. Aside from a general, well-hidden cache of arms, many individuals were also privately armed. In the past year, they had initiated a few raids, mostly on jails in remote towns in which their own people were incarcerated, or in support of strike attempts by KMU unions in Davao City. They had killed two Filipino soldiers at an outpost they declined to name, but in general they were an armed force prepared for insurrection, working toward a takeover against Marcos. They asked if Gene thought Ninoy Aquino would be a good leader for the Philippines, or if he were too much of an aristocrat to work with village people for land reform. Did Gene know Aquino had been removed from jail in the Philippines only because his heart had started to fail? Did he know that Imelda Marcos was behind Ninoy's release, fearing the withdrawal of American bases if he died?

Once Gene grew accustomed to the M-16s and automatic weapons, these people reminded him of folks from Wapato, or Uncle Leo's barrio. He respected them for their intent and seriousness, but also detected a forced bravado in their tough jungle talk. Julio drove him home over a heaving road at three o'clock in the morning, drunk on beer and words. "Someday," Julio said, "I hope to go to the States myself."

❊

Gene set out on his own to discover the remoteness of Philippine life. He headed north and northwest by bus after first flying to Manila, then following the coast of the Lingayen Gulf. He checked into a two-room hotel near the highway. The owner, who operated from a creaking bamboo wheelchair, advised Gene of remote, inexpensive places and trustworthy jeepney drivers, and outlined a route all the way to Santo Fernando through a crisscross of dirt roads and outback villages. He also warned Gene of HUKs in the woods, insisting that there were remnants of armed guerrilla armies that had survived World War II, men who had never gotten word that they were extinct.

Gene asked, "Weren't they the loyal ones? They fought the Japanese army."

The old man answered, "You bet. I was one of them." He sucked on his dying cigar and patted his forty-year-old thigh wound.

Gene left the following day, traveling with drivers who usually knew a smattering of English. Trekking into the most remote jungle outposts, the jeepneys whined along dense trails; when the trails became impassable, Gene switched to horses. He cherished these journeys, plowing through tangled foliage and pastoral clearings, above which waterfalls dropped hundreds of meters.

The further Gene moved into village life, the less striking the poverty. At first the sight of people living alongside their chickens and livestock wrenched his gut, but he quickly grew used to it. He did not feel indifferent to the plight of these people so much as tempted to join them. Given the chance, he consistently overtipped and overpaid, but he did not change his pants or shirt for days on end. He scarcely noticed when rips opened up in his worn jeans and sleeves tore away from his shirt, enabling him to cool his armpits like a cormorant drying its wings. On rare occasion when his room included a mirror, he faltered before it, wondering who was that black man in front of him. And the man he became on this northern trip sank so deeply into his consciousness that he lay at night under torn netting, thinking how close he had come to being the dark man he feared as a child.

Gene

We walk the streets this man and I hungry looking for a place to eat one of us pointing to a tilted house who is the man I almost know like a word on the edge of my tongue he's climbing coiled iron stairs up and up to the top of the house we enter a room not a room my own skull light blazing within I wake up suddenly as if someone the jeepney man the innkeeper has slipped into bed beside me sleeping bag drenched with sweat it's me it is me I have become one with my own duality.

Gene took comfort in this newly discovered darker side of himself. Two weeks passed and he moved with increasing ease from village to village, the dialect passing into Ilocano, more familar to him than Tagalog because it was the language of his father. The fruit tasted sweeter and more succulent and the local beers left a delicious tang on his gums. He ate soft-shell crabs, carapace and all; iodine-flavored seaweed he learned to prefer to lettuce.

Late one day, wearing the straw hat his uncle Manuelo had given him, now christened with dust from the road, a few fronds missing, Gene set off once more on horseback. The guides, noting his quietness, rode a respectable distance ahead. Moving along a trail only yards from the beach and sea, Gene was wrapped in thought. I wonder if I'll ever meet Friday.

He rode a few steps farther, stunned. Until this solo journey, he had always thought of himself as Crusoe, the white man! He repeated the words aloud. "I wonder if I'll ever meet Friday." The native islander. How could he have missed the fact that day after day, he was coming closer to himself, Viernes, Friday? Immediately he knew he had to change course and head south again to find Luis, to locate his union mission and return to his work with his newly integrated whole self.

Riding back to Bulacan on the bus, the sun beating against his face, Gene felt his village identity slipping away. But he did not judge himself for the metamorphosis; he had responsibilities waiting that had to be met.

As Gene watched the countryside speed by, he realized the brevity of his six-week stay, and began to suffer withdrawal. If religious, right now he'd be bartering with God. "Lord, don't take this beautiful place away from me. You must not remove it from my guts and soul." And the Lord might respond, "We'll comprise." Then he'd ask, "Arbitration?" "All right," God would say. "You can't stay, but the impressions you took on this trip will last the rest of your life."

❈

Days later, as Gene was clearing Customs in Hawaii, a young, tanned officer in a crisp white uniform shirt glanced from his passport to a computer sheet beside her. "Mr. Viernes?" she asked, lowering her voice protectively. "Would you mind stepping through that door over there?" She pointed toward a bank of glass-fronted offices. "Just a couple of questions, that fellow in there from the Immigration and Naturalization Service. Won't take too long." She flashed a professional smile across a face otherwise devoid of emotion.

Seattle
April-May 1981
Honolulu
March-May 1981

Silme missed Gene while he was in the Philippines, despite being

93

surrounded almost constantly by dozens of other friends and associates. People who knew Silme often remarked how they envied his easy way of making contacts and winning support. One lazy Sunday morning, Terri told him, "They'll make you mayor, the way you bridge gaps."

"Yeah," he said, the pillow muffling his words, "but I'd rather be mayor of the ID."

She jumped on his back. "That's what I meant, fool. God, the ego! You didn't think I meant the whole city?" He tried to roll her off, but she howled and they heard Ligaya as she came running down the hall. "Stay in bed, your majesty," Terri said, pulling on her sweat clothes. "I'll bring you coffee and the paper."

"Hey, no less than I deserve—especially if I join Dimas Alang," he added, naming a conservative Filipino lodge to which every ID businessman interested in power belonged.

"Somehow I can't see you in a little red hat with a tassle," she laughed from the kitchen.

Despite occasional setbacks, Silme and Terri's relationship improved steadily as they planned their trip to Hawaii. They had made another major commitment to each other with a second child, a girl, Kalayaan, and planned somehow to buy a house. From time to time Terri had to face Silme's longing for a bachelor life, but she noted that he had been drinking less and was now spending more time at home than in the Four Seas. They were both treated fondly by their respective parents, and intended to get married when they returned from Hawaii.

Now lying on his back in a tangle of sheets, listening to the late April rain, Silme unfolded and re-read Gene's letter, puzzling over Gene's reference to someone he had met who was "native." Silme wondered if Gene was experiencing the same almost mystical phenomenon he had felt on his trip to the Philippines with his father in 1972. But Silme had been very young and was just becoming politically aware at the time; he'd thrown aside his experience as irrational voodoo. Now he envied Gene's chance at self-discovery, and missed him twice as much.

When Terri came back with his coffee, Silme doubled up under the sheets, then rolled abruptly to his side, pretending to be shot. He groaned and Terri brought the cup down heavily on the nightstand, coffee sloshing over the rim. "Bastard," she muttered, and left the room.

Silme asked Gene, across the Pacific, "Was that my darker side coming out?" He drank his coffee, dressed, and when he found Terri in the kitchen, held her close, his face buried in her neck.

"Why did you do that?" she asked.

❀

With the help of Gene's letters which detailed the facts Olalia and Beltran wished Local 37 to include in their resolution, Silme and Terri worked long nights with the executive committee before putting the final draft to the rank and file. The rank and file voted to pass the resolution over Tony Baruso's blustering opposition.

Unions in the US had rarely declared themselves so boldly international in focus. Their resolution, in which International Longshore Workers supported the cessation of anti-union measures in the Philippines, had few precedents. Local 37's resolution statistically recorded the average earned incomes of families in the Philippines and what they paid for food. It revealed Marcos's decrees against strikes and any wage increases not sanctioned by his office, as well as his outrageous military expenditures. It also focused on the Philippines' double-digit inflation rate.

But the resolution's strongest point was the recognition of the KMU as the main organization representing labor in the Philippines. As a follow-up measure, the resolution proposed that the union would periodically send delegates from the ILWU to the Philippines to monitor labor conditions under martial law. The overall lofty, but not impossible, goals of the resolution were to raise working conditions and wages, make the Philippines a better place to live, and dam the conduit of cheap, menial labor that flowed out to Hong Kong, the United States, and western Europe.

Given the political climate in the US and Philippines in 1981, Silme and Terri could not imagine taking a more revolutionary stand. So it seemed odd to them to fly into a tropical paradise, wear leis of heady plumeria blossoms, and book a room at the Sheraton Waikiki, where the convention was to be held. After only two nights in the place, Terri, Silme and Cindy—having already blown their budget on room service—packed their bags and moved out.

As they dragged their bags across the lobby of the Sheraton, Silme spied Gene grinning at them across the room. Silme moved quickly. "Gene," he said, embracing him, "are you that tan all over?"

"Nah, it's just a farm boy's tan, you know me." Gene grinned again but Silme noted his friend's eyes darting warily around the large room. He struck Gene's chest.

"Man, you been workin' out?"

"This is the real me," Gene said as he hugged Cindy and Terri.

The four friends grabbed a cab and found another hotel, where they rented a room with two double beds and two portable cots, a bargain at forty dollars a night. Then they headed for a bar near the beach and a final discussion of strategy before putting the resolution before a committee vote.

Seated in a booth, they drank orange juice and coffee. Gene said casually, "I got red-flagged when I landed here. My name's on a 'national security' print-out."

"What do they do?" Cindy asked.

Gene shrugged. "The INS isn't too smooth. 'Why did you fly to the Philippines? Who did you see there? What is your business in Hawaii?' I just told them what I did, asked if there's a law against it. They gave me real straight looks and said, 'No, no law, just watch it.' That was it. Fuck'em. It's all connected. I had to call Geline from a booth last night because I didn't trust the phone in my room."

"Do you think you're being followed?" Terri asked.

"Did you notice how fast I moved you all into that cab?" Gene grinned. "Not bad, huh?"

"Not this game again." Cindy brought her hands up to her head and rubbed her temples.

Gene leaned back, his profile dark against the strong spring sun. Waves crashed on the beach. "We're playing it," he said quietly. "What else can we do? When we start this resolution, we'll really be in deep shit."

"Automatically?" Silme wondered.

"Maybe already. No, I don't think anyone tagged me out of the hotel. But I'm not staying there, and maybe I'll move in with you tonight, someone else tomorrow."

The juke box buzzed in the late morning quiet and the bartender, a Hawaiian woman, talked softly to a customer at the bar. What little light filtered into the room caused everyone to appear as silhouettes, cutouts of the tourists or honeymooners they might have been in another lifetime. For the first time Silme realized what, more than anything, was keeping Gene single: his deep sense of the gravity of their lives. Gene hadn't needed to be in Nazario's driveway to see him gunned down to pass into this zone of fatal knowledge.

"Well," Silme said, "we better get down to the nuts and bolts of this resolution before we take it to committee. If we get a pass on it there, the voice vote on the floor should follow pretty easily."

"Where does Local 142 stand?" Terri asked Gene.

"I met with their president, Carl Damasco. He's an older guy, very aware of real conditions in the Philippines. I spent four hours with him last night, two the night before. I think he favors the resolution."

"That's amazing." Terri sat back, shaking her head with disbelief. "Because from what I hear of that union, they never break rank! The majority goes along with the leader."

"But they've got two really tough guys in there, Benny Quitevis and Bert Alcaraz, both tight with Marcos," Gene pointed out. "We'll meet them in committee soon enough. I heard they've been trying to drum up votes against the resolution for days now."

"How did they know about it so soon?" Cindy asked.

"Either Baruso informed them or someone who worked on the resolution isn't as progressive as he claims to be," Terri put in.

"Who do you mean?" Gene asked.

"Baruso's got this condo over here," Terri explained. "Abe Cruz worked closely with us in Seattle but is now inviting us all over to Tony's for 'a drink and steaks,' telling us how 'well stocked' the place is. Like we can all be friends!"

"Where does Baruso stand?" Gene asked.

"He was shouting us down the whole time we were planning this trip," Terri told Gene, "saying the resolution was pro-Communist. The usual shit. Then over the last week or so, he calmed down. We know that he wrote to the International, asking to be named a delegate if the resolution passes."

"So if he goes to the Philippines to inspect the labor situation firsthand," Gene anticipated, "he comes back with glowing reports."

"The guy is slick," Silme said.

"But people in the International know him," Terri insisted. "They haven't even answered him. He thinks silence means acceptance."

"How do you know that?" Cindy asked.

Terri laughed. "From Abe Cruz, of course, after he came back drunk from Tony's condo last night! Okay, now, enough gossip." she pushed them. "Are we going for this?"

"The whole way." Gene sliced his hand through the air. "What have we got to lose?"

As the women led the way out of the bar, Gene grabbed Silme's elbow to slow him down. He asked quietly, "Anything more on who got Nazario?"

Silme shook his head. "Leads that go nowhere."

"Any connection with Baruso?"

"Not much. He's more visible here than he was in Seattle, and he's tight with the biggest Honolulu operators—they like him. He's got a security clearance from the State Department. I figure he's telling the honchos in the Hawaiian unions that he can eventually deliver us."

Gene slipped his hand into Silme's and squeezed hard, remembering their days of innocence when their greatest challenges took place on amateur wrestling mats.

❖

The International Longshoremen's and Warehousemen's Union Convention generated the power of politics in a carnival atmosphere. Delegates with name tags pinned to parrot-plumed chests reveled in celebratory fashion in a high-class hotel meeting hall that made everyone feel they mattered. Some of the men present were old enough to remember convening in places like the Crater Hotel in Klamath Falls, Oregon, in roach-infested rooms with bed linens reeking of tobacco. In the fifties, longshoremen wore snap-brims and double-breasted suits to their conventions. Here at the Sheraton tanned men and women in bright shirts and pastel slacks grinned behind icy cans of Budweiser and screwdrivers with plastic swizzle sticks. But neither the air of gaiety nor the costumes detracted from the message of the delegates' firm, lingering handshakes—their seriousness of purpose and desire for unity with brother and sister workers across the Pacific.

By the very nature of being Filipino, most at the ILWU gathering were deeply connected to their homeland. But while they had backed progressive union sanctions against dictatorships in other countries and apartheid in South Africa, they were hopelessly split over denouncing the Marcos regime. The Hawaiian convention turned out to be the dirtiest, toughest, strangest experience the Seattle members had ever known.

Before taking the floor, while the resolution was still in committee, Quitevis and Alcaraz refused to talk about Marcos' record, saying it was irrelevant. "No union has any business doing anything but business!" someone remarked from the back of the Hospitality Room.

"'A union's business is business?' That sounds like Dave Beck!" Silme spoke out.

"Who the hell's that?" the man asked scornfully. "You can't mess with what's going on in another country!"

Gene rose to his feet. "What is going on in another country? You want stats, I'll give you stats."

"You don't know shit. You been there once, you don't see shit. Marcos built roads and schools, he kept the Communists out!"

"Yeah, too long," another delegate shouted.

The man screamed, "You wouldn't talk that shit in the Philippines!"

"Yeah, we'd have trouble talking at all!" Gene interrupted. "You want goddamn Communists running this union, go ahead and give the KMU clout and see what happens. Whose side you fuckin' on?"

"Marcos built up his own army to put down unions," Gene shouted back. "We're unions, he's not! Jesus Christ, under martial law you can't strike! You want that for this union? Who's side you fuckin' on?"

Carl Damasco, silver-haired and dignified in a pale blue suit, stood with both hands raised. "Please, gentlemen, may we hear the resolution? Let's get it read, at least. Brother Domingo?" He turned toward Silme, who came to the podium. Tony Baruso sat with Quitevis and Alcaraz, trying to calm them, but eyeing Gene angrily for his outburst.

"Since martial law," Silme began, "the average pay has dropped by thirty-nine percent in seven years. Sixty-five percent of firms in the Philippines, by their own admission, are in violation of wage, health and safety standards. Thirty-eight labor leaders have either disappeared or been 'salvaged' under the Marcos regime—"

"What the hell does that mean?"

Silme held a restraining hand toward Gene who had begun to push out of his seat in anger. "I think you know damn well what it means. Either murdered—"

"Bullshit!"

"—murdered or tortured into taking a pro-Marcos stand. Hundreds more labor leaders were thrown in jail. Despite the official lifting of martial law, no alterations have been made in repressive labor practices."

"You just said it, 'the official lifting of martial law'!"

"Which was whitewash," Gene pointed out, "for some American diplomat handing over more money for the military bases!"

"Where does he get that shit?" Baruso muttered.

Silme continued to speak in an attempt to sharpen the committee's understanding of the document. Sensitive to the fact that most of the delegates were Filipinos, he insisted that the resolution did not condemn the Philippine government. "It would be irresponsible for us as a union, given the importance of our relationship to the home country, to avoid passing this resolution."

Ever the diplomat, Silme received a warm round of applause from the majority of the committee members. After two more hours of acrimonious debate, redbaiting, and cursing, the committee voted to pass the resolution onto the floor of the convention.

❦

On the floor itself, ILWU President Jim Herman presided with ex-officio Harry Bridges by his side, watching for parliamentary gaffes.

When Tony Baruso took the microphone, he followed a predictable path. "This resolution never will in any way attempt to condemn the Marcos regime as martial law," he said in his expansive, confident way. "To the contrary, we respect the wishes of the majority of the forty-seven million people in the country for accepting martial law. I do hope my countrymen who are members of Hawaiian Local 142 understand that we are only interested as trade unionists in this part of the world, to have a look-see and maybe we could help—with the expertise of this union—the suffering brothers and sisters back home.

"I have been selected to the International Executive Board, and more than once traveled over the length and breadth of my home country, meeting everyone from servant to aristocrat. I have to say the civil rights and also the trade union wages are low, and if this resolution passes, remember that it comes out of my office, because I am both president and business agent of Local 37. If it's implemented, I'll be behind that process, too." Silme and Gene exchanged warning glances, noting the way Tony was preparing a way for the resolution to work for him and his cohorts.

Gene took the floor, breathing deeply to calm himself. "As Tony has pointed out, despite the resolution's format, we are not calling for a condemnation of the Marcos government. We only advocate that this issue be aired. Now, the main source of information in the United States carries a distinct bias towards the Marcos government, and a bias presented by the US State Department. There are people like myself who would like to see other views expressed. This resolution gives us a concrete way to educate our members, our community, and hopefully, other trade unions."

Gene went on to talk about the problems the unions faced in organizing Filipino workers in the US, citing several unfavorable myths generated by those who hired them: that Filipinos are unorganizable, that they scab and happily agree to slave wages. "This resolution is aimed at providing information to our membership about conditions in the Philippines that cause, every year, thirty to forty thousand Filipinos to migrate to the US—conditions that create an ideal climate for runaway shops—and about how workers in the Philippines are trying to raise their wages despite extremely difficult conditions."

Gene implored the delegates to visualize the resolution as a means for finding solutions to these labor problems. "With the answers I not only hope to add to my effectiveness as a leader, but to Local 37's effectiveness in becoming a stronger and more capable union." Then he offered the chair a letter addressed to the convention from Bert Ayala and Ernesto Arillano, two outlawed labor leaders from the Philippines, calling for solidarity.

As President Herman gaveled down jeers and applause, Gene stood for a moment, believing with the deepest conviction that he and his friends had won. When Bart Alcaraz came to the podium, he tossed one smoldering look Gene's way before facing the audience, the majority of whom now sat back in their chairs with arms folded across their chests.

Although Alcaraz said he spoke in favor of the resolution, he proceeded to insist that rice production had risen so remarkably under Marcos's rule that the "people in the barrios are now the richest of all. My brothers who are left behind, and sisters, are beneficiaries of the new society.

"Lastly, if you read the newspapers, ninety-seven percent voted yes, in favor of the Marcos administration. When Marcos opted for martial law, he brought with him a mandate of forty-seven million Filipinos. I support Marcos not because he is my godfather but because millions of Filipinos have benefited from his rule."

Alcaraz took his seat and Tony Baruso came forward once more, still clapping for his friend. "Let the record show," he spoke loudly, "that I have been a national guest. Yours truly was invited to the Philippines to look and see the real life of the Filipinos. I am not contending that I know every goddamn thing there—I don't. But the only thing I am saying is that the life of the working people, the wages, could be better. We are not objecting to martial law, we are only objecting to some sanctions—"

President Herman interrupted to remind Baruso of his time limit.

"That is the essence of this particular resolution," Baruso said hurriedly. "I repeat, we are not here to condemn what I myself and my family in the Philippines are enjoying. Brother Chairman," he suddenly put forward, "I move to close the debate."

This last remark brought forth laughter and applause. The favorable voice vote that followed was almost an anticlimax. Gene and Silme couldn't help but admire Baruso's move; it was clear how he had lasted so long at this game. But while Baruso knew exactly how to appear to favor both sides simultaneously, what he might have to answer to violence-prone Marcos supporters in the next few days was anyone's guess.

Silme

People in and out of room until early morning hours now I can't sleep think of Ligaya Kalyaan at my mother's exhausted trying to figure out how the hardliners see the meeting a blow against a sick benevolent leader or if they go along with the resolution do they worry they'll be seen as enemies of Filipinos light striking the blinds already morning even winning I need more sleep than this damned insomnia plaguing me for months hear Gene's breathing Cindy's arm dangling from her cot touch Terri's back she gives a tiny gasp strange sensation someone extra in the room a huge roach tank body green-gold-black stalking down the wall slide out of bed pick up my shoe watch it crawl on desk heading toward draft of resolution slam it hard.

"What's that?" Gene startled in his sleep. Silme said nothing, wiped his shoe on the rug and returned to bed.

❧

The next day Baruso surprised Silme with a call, inviting "all of you people" to luncheon at an expensive Japanese restaurant. Silme put his hand over the phone. "Terri, he says he wants you, me, Cindy, Gene—"

"—no way," Gene offered from his cot.

"He says the whole thing's on him and the Dimas Alang. What should I say?"

Terri reminded him they were broke and hungry. "Go ahead and accept."

Three hours later the three who had gone to the luncheon met Gene for a farewell drink at Honolulu International Airport. Gene's flight was leaving later, returning via Anchorage. "Did Baruso really expect me to show?" Gene asked. "He hates my guts and the feeling's mutual."

"He acted so strange," Terri said, pouring beer into her glass. "He seemed really pissed that you didn't come."

"'That goddamn Viernes,'" Cindy imitated. "'He turns down a classy place like the Jade Pagoda. That farm boy! Shitkicker!'"

"All these Filipino guys were there we'd never seen before," Silme explained. "Then the photo routine again, just like Montoya. Taking my picture, me with Terri, Cindy and me, Cindy and Terri. Snapping the fish in the ponds, the little cabana we ate in. Food was pretty good, though—butterfly prawns."

Cindy laughed. "When we were done eating, he said, 'okay, girls, the men got to talk alone, this is a lodge meeting, you can go shopping!' For a minute I thought he was going to give Terri and me money and tell us what to buy."

"It was Dimas Alang, then?" Gene asked.

"Yeah," Silme nodded. "After Cindy and Terri left, all these guys, including Baruso and my dad, started talking in Ilocano. I couldn't follow any of it, and I kept wondering what the hell I was supposed to understand by this display. Some kind of vague threat? Like the old ways, the old language still controls? Later, Baruso left, mumbling something about staying longer in Hawaii, and my dad's staying here with my sister Lynn for the rest of the week. So, here we are."

"Weird," Gene said. "But in a day or so it'll be business as usual back at the office."

"That's our flight," Terri said, and kissed Gene goodbye.

103

Seattle, Wapato, Vancouver Island
Late May 1981

A week later, in Seattle, Gene jogged from KDP headquarters to Terri and Silme's apartment to avoid using his truck. The day before he had noted a blue car tagging him. He also suspected that the headquarters' phone was bugged and the union hall was being watched. Gene wanted out of town.

Friday after work, he drove headlong over the Cascades, turned right in Ellensburg, crested the Manashtash and coasted all the way down the ridge, home for the second time since his trip to Hawaii. His hand gripped the steering wheel like a vise, and a muscle jumped nervously in his neck. He was anxious to find Andy, whom he had missed on his last visit, but he was more anxious about the scene he had left behind in Seattle.

Gene was seated on his friend's front steps, drinking a beer with Andy's brother, John, when Andy pulled up in his Plymouth, home from work.

"Jesus Christ," Andy said, moving toward Gene like a truck. He gripped Gene hard. "I ain't seen you in a hundred years."

"Yeah. Hawaii, you heard?"

"You left out the Philippines," John said. The two brothers laughed, but Gene realized the distance he put between the two places that for him were like paradise and hell.

"Yeah," Gene said apologetically. "You wouldn't have any money, would you, Andy?"

Andy leaned forward. "How much you need?"

"No, I've got money. I mean for yourself?"

"I just got paid."

"Road trip?"

Andy moved immediately toward the house. "Two minutes to pack," he threw over his shoulder.

❧

It took a long time for darkness to fall, for Gene to slake the coals of his life in the city. Andy tried unsuccessfully to get him to talk. "Where're we heading, besides north?" he asked quietly from the passenger side.

"I don't know, maybe Glen's place."

Andy whistled. "This is big time, huh? I called in sick for Monday at the last stop, just in case."

"I would've phoned home myself if my phone wasn't bugged."

"What? Be real."

It had been months since the two old friends had talked. Gene panicked momentarily with the eerie thought of losing his closest companion, the guy with whom he had first feasted and shared secrets. He remembered Andy standing across from him at the cannery fish tables at two in the morning, their hands trembling from Dexadrine, the old men sleeping behind them, propped against the wall with sacks over their heads. Gene told him what he was thinking.

"We were insane," Andy whispered hoarsely as they hurtled through White Pass, taking the southern route to Seattle. Gene looked in the rearview mirror; there were no other cars in sight. He exhaled.

"What's this about your phone?" Andy asked.

"Every time we lift it there's a click. So we've got codes. Call a guy up, if he thinks there's something nasty coming down, he talks about temperature; if he talks about wind, things are clear."

"Sounds like fucking James Bond."

"Wish it didn't."

Trees lined the road, their tops still glowing with the setting sun. A semi slashed past in the other direction.

"What the hell are you into, Gene? The word is all over down here, all over the city when I was up there last month, that you're in deep shit. When that guy Nazario got killed, I just heard 'dispatcher' and thought it was you!"

"Close, huh?" Gene said sadly. He saw poor Naz, spinning in his driveway, bullets cutting the air.

"What is this guy Baruso doing? I hear bad things."

"He's just another old man." Gene shook his head. "Look, Andy, I started in a direction and I can't stop."

"I guess so." Andy was quiet for a mile or two. They passed a sign for Enumclaw. "You could always come home."

Gene did not answer.

"Is that so bad? Down here we're all your friends, we'd cover you all the time."

Gene waved a hand briefly from the wheel. "I've left."

"No way," Andy insisted. "You don't leave until we say you can.

Since when is Seattle better?"

"It's not Seattle. It's not home, the farm, Wapato, you guys. I left. I went in deep. When you go in deep you don't come out, and you sure as hell don't go home."

"If you're gonna get heavy on me, we need a six, maybe a twelve. There's a store up there, see the lights?"

Standing behind the men's room with bottles of Rainier, they stretched and breathed in the May mountain air. Gene punched Andy on the arm. "Maybe I should take up something more strenuous than jogging," he said. "You're not flabby at all."

"Heck no." Andy pumped his bicep. "Gorgeous George."

Gene laughed, remembering a day they had toured the Yakima Business College gym, checking out future opponents. If it were only that easy to check out his enemies now, or to know who was checking on him. Where did they meet? What did they say? Who was talking?

"Hey, buddy." Andy's brow deepened. "Your face is going through all these contortions, you aware of that?"

"Tics," Gene offered. "Come on, your turn to drive."

For a long while they quit talking. The silence was pleasant. Occasionally they stopped to drink another beer or relieve themselves behind a tree. They roared past Seattle in the dark, with mutual relief, bypassing the place where Gene worked and slept. When they passed through Mount Vernon an hour later, Andy said, "I have a job here, helping migrant workers. State-funded. They're building a low-cost housing unit over there."

He pointed east toward the Cascade Mountains. "Day care, all that good stuff. Hard to believe I'll be doing what I trained for in college."

"What were we trained for?" Gene mused, then added, "God, I just remembered Skip. You knew he died of cancer?"

"And other things. I was at the funeral."

"Wasn't the healthiest guy," Gene said, his voice opening in tribute, "except in the head."

"Hey," Andy said quietly, "he signaled us through a lot of flak. We didn't even know we were a minority until we met him." The two men laughed, each remembering their college days. As they continued north, they talked of Andy's divorce and children, his chance to relocate.

At the Canadian border, the white monument dedicated to "children of a common parent" glazed in moonlight reflecting off

106

the water. The border guard asked the usual questions and they proceeded across.

They checked into the Palace Hotel on Pender, near Vancouver's skid road. It was close to eleven when they each bought a beer in the enormous lobby bar. Only four other people sat in the smoky, old-time, red plush room. Gene stared across the room at a slender, dark woman in a red sheath: it was Leila. As soon as he saw her partner wobble off to the men's room, he got up and walked in her direction. "Are you in as good shape as he's in?" he asked.

Leila looked up, startled, and smiled widely. "Gene."

"Good memory."

She patted the guy's empty chair but Gene shook his head.

"What you been doin' all this time, I heard you went—"

Gene put his finger to his lips. "I'm in Room 301," he said, his eyes not leaving hers.

Leila tilted her head away from him. "Okay, I'll ditch him. Soon."

Back at the table with Andy, he tried to explain his feelings for Leila. "How could I know she'd be here?" Gene said. "Well, yeah," Andy sighed, "but couldn't she have a friend?" "If she does, we'll come straight back," Gene promised. "You understand?" He squeezed Andy's shoulder before hurrying off to the elevator. Leila stood waiting in front of his door. Fumbling for the key, he held her in an awkward hug.

"Hey, wait," she protested, "I can't do this. Come over to my place, walk me around the block. Be romantic."

After an hour-long ferry ride to the north shore and back and a walk around the block stepping over drunks, Leila and Gene held each other at her door. "This is another uncle," she whispered, and Gene started to laugh. "Okay ... I'm married. I moved up. Got a cannery job. I remembered you when I got it. Only this one's non-union. That's what my booger-nose husband does when he ain't drunk. He dispatches from a room down at the Palace." She squinted her eyes critically. "You were good to me but you ain't changed."

"Probably not," Gene agreed.

"Your head is always somewhere else," she said pensively. She bent to pluck a blossom of the mock orange next to the door and pinned it in her black hair. The scent reminded him of the Philippines. "It's okay. It's just you. Tonight when I saw you walk across the floor, I thought, 'who the hell he think he is, so cocky.'" She cupped his crotch playfully. "And your eyes so bright when you looked at me and I saw it was you again."

Gene touched Leila's chin and tried to kiss her, but she pushed away.

"No, no. You could never mean it. Don't look that way. I could love you but you could never. Gotta go, feel a little sick. Don't forget, two blocks that way, you can get a cab—"

Suddenly she kissed him. She grabbed his hand and led him into the house. He stood in a living room lit by moonlight. She whispered from another room and when he found her, she was unzipping her dress.

"This your bedroom?"

"So what?" She unbuckled his belt.

"Naw, come on, the living room." He pulled her gently.

Five minutes later, her breasts crushed soft against his chest as they lay on the couch, two shafts of headlight probed the ceiling and the plaster walls of the room. Gene rammed his bare feet into his shoes and gunned on his pants, jamming his underwear into his pocket.

Leila thrust his jacket toward him. "Take this, it's cold," she said calmly and led him to the back of the house. "This way, down those stairs."

He grabbed her hand and squeezed hard.

"Kiss," she said. "Call me!"

"Who? Where? Where do I go?"

"Up the alley." She pointed. "Two blocks. I'm Curry, in the book."

❋

The next morning Gene apologized to Andy by buying his hash browns, eggs, and Canadian bacon. They lingered over their coffee, planning their trip, before walking eastward through a gentrified Gas Town, once Vancouver's skid road district and the center of the city's origins. Gene bought a book on the history of North Pacific fisheries that included a photo of an Iron Chink. They took a bus to Stanley Park and walked a path through old-growth cedars to the aquarium where they watched otters slide from their mock-castle home into the moat. "Look!" Andy said, as one of the otters, swimming on its back, cracked a crab against a rock on its chest.

"I remember them from Alaska," Gene said fondly.

❋

That night at the Palace, sitting in leather chairs with four Molsons in front of them on the table, Andy broke into their vacation mood. "Why are you doing this dangerous work? Make me understand— I'm just not political."

"Am I?" Gene wondered. "I don't know. I started because I felt pushed in Alaska. Maybe I should never have felt that. Once I began, I grew desperate about doing the right thing. I read about our history, started writing. Maybe I shouldn't have read certain material. Now I'm here."

"But, Gene, the guys who got Nazario are real gangsters, they have real guns. What should we do?"

"What do you mean, 'what should we do?'"

"You want us to shoot them, or what? Beat the shit out of them? Point out who's harrassing you. Who the hell is Baruso and these other assholes?"

"Forget it. If we went after them, we'd be playing their game. We've never resorted to violence, and besides, they always win that game."

Andy's face moved close to Gene's as he leaned forward to reach his beer. "Come home."

"Come on, Andy, what am I supposed to do there? I have a job, I have to dispatch."

"There's bad rumors."

"Yeah, well." Gene felt a throbbing in the side of his neck. He got up from the table and walked around the room, pausing before the pay phone, anxiety knotting his stomach in a way that had become all too familiar these days. Who am I supposed to call? What if this phone is bugged? He rubbed his neck and exhaled deeply. You're on the road. There's no one you need to speak to. Relax. He slumped down beside his friend.

"You could go back to the way you were," Andy insisted, creaking in the leather chair. "Can't you undo things?"

"I don't think you believe that, Andy. Would you go back on the divorce?"

Andy was silent.

"Look, friend," Gene continued, "I went as far back as I could in the Philippines, and now it's all over me like a scent." "You could get out, go to New York," Andy said. "What difference would it make? Or just stay right here ... hey, with that beautiful girl."

"I wondered when you'd get to her again—thanks, I deserved that. I couldn't stay here. You got to understand, I didn't intend to make trouble for myself, neither did Silme. Trouble was waiting for us when we got to Hawaii, and it's all around us now."

"We'll beat 'em up."

Gene choked down a painful laugh, remembering how often Andy had said this in their youth. "Who do you look for? They're agents, Andy. Folks working for both Marcos and our government, which is colluding with that pig dictator. Agents were right there in Hawaii, among the delegates."

"Jesus." Andy looked away a long time, his brow scrunched. Finally he said, "You shouldn't have gone."

"Andy, I went. It's done. And now the people in the KDP are being followed—three or four of us, anyway."

Andy shook his head forlornly. "Yeah, well, like you say, it's done. You went." Sadness had replaced the sarcasm in his voice; he was beginning to understand his friend's dilemma.

"What are you trying to build, Andy?"

"A scene like yours, but more connected with the state, the feds. The union stuff is good for migrant worker protection. But housing first."

"We weren't doing anything all that different."

"KDP? I don't know. I think I'm two or three minorities. I've been getting involved with La Paloma. Hispanic."

"Well, their needs are the same as ours, and our parents'."

"Ah, well," Andy sighed. "Think we can stay up late tonight and still drive to Glen's tomorrow?"

"Aye aye, captain," Gene said. Andy winked and pretended to pull a skipper's hat tight on his head.

❊

It was a fast ferry ride across the Georgia Straits to Vancouver Island, through a southwest wind that kicked up clouds and a spray of late spring rain. A drive north and two more tiny ferries later, they were on Hornby Island, alive with wild roses and birds. Rhododendrons drooped purple and wild azaleas burned orange, while the copper bark of madrona trees rose to clutches of red berries and oval leaves. An occasional opening in the tall evergreens bordering the road revealed the sea sculpted by the wind into white, peaked waves.

Andy shook his head as he drove. "How is this place possible in a world full of exhaust and filth?"

As Gene shook Glen's hand, he felt a stab of envy for his brother's solidity and self-confidence. Then, hugging Adele, Glen's wife, he thought briefly of Leila. Adele was tall, slim and white, with brown hair falling to her shoulders. A boy and girl raced up to grab Gene and Andy, ready to play. Gene thought of his uncle's place in Tuloan. Glen's uncle, too, he reminded himself.

"You're nearly as dark now as I am," Glen said warmly.

"Hey, I'm losing it," Gene insisted.

On the kitchen table lay a Haida puppet, nearly life-size. Its primary color was a soft green; the limbs moved realistically, the joints controlled by an intricate system of leather thongs. "I always wondered how you got so far, coming off that little farm in Parker. Were there any art classes in high school?" Gene asked.

Glen looked at Gene blankly. "You know," he said, puzzled, "I don't know." He turned toward Adele.

"Don't ask me," she said. "I wasn't there. I don't even know where Parker is."

"Don't go home much, brother?"

"Has it been that long?" Glen asked Adele, looking rueful.

"Glen, you've never even taken me to Parker, wherever it is."

"No, no, no," Glen said, relieved. "Parker's just up the road from Wapato. We went there after our wedding."

"We did? Oh, yeah," Adele said, "the time I met your mom and sis."

Late into the evening, Gene's niece, ignoring hints that she and her little brother ought to go to bed, demanded one more story about the Philippines. Gene had already described the ghetto near the Cultural Center, and the children running wildly around at the pig roast at his uncle's place. Glen and Adele's boy, not yet in kindergarten, asked, "They go to school?" Gene said he doubted it.

Glen leaned towards Gene, fascinated. "I never think of myself as Filipino," he said. "Maybe I should. They carve great masks."

"What's Filipino?" Gene's nephew asked. His dad and Andy smiled.

"That's it for tonight, kids—time for bed," Adele laughed.

But later, after Gene had tiptoed into the children's room to crawl into his sleeping bag, his niece whispered loudly, "How big's a water buffalo?"

Gene

Loud insistent ring someone calling me I look up dark phone within reach on wall move slowly across matted rug bogged down by ancient suit of armor feel vulnerable must answer the ring compelling me draw closer reach out heavy metal arm ringing stops but phone moans a name I drop the receiver phone becomes a carved mask mouth huge pouting lips moaning moaning black eyes crimson retinas penetrate my own—

Gene and Andy stayed a couple of days, the best part scouring the beach for butter clams. Gene felt the island's charm not only in the hunt for clams but in the way the entire party relaxed with what this place had offered as far back as time reached. The next day, as the adults shucked oysters, the children hooted from the tops of sand cliffs before tumbling to the kelp-covered beach.

Soon after they left Hornby, spinning south through the glare of interstate traffic, Andy and Gene felt the weekend drawing down, their work rising to meet them. But Gene hoped to carry home some of the pleasure he had felt on the island, in the presence of his friend, his brother and his family.

He hugged Andy good-bye. "Andy, you are the best. Good trip, man."

Andy smiled. Then he, too, was a long way down the road.

❊

Life under the new dispatch system promised instant conflict. In late May, Tony Dictado, gambling boss at the Golden Dragon Restaurant, walked into Gene's office. A hefty man about the same age as Gene, Dictado worked with the Tulisan and was friendly with Baruso. The scent of his cologne rolled into the corners of the office. Smoothing his thin, drop-down mustache, he began to fire off the names of men he wanted to have sent to the canneries.

"They got seniority?" Gene asked.

"Fuck seniority," Dictado said. "What is that?"

"You know what it is, Tony, our new system. So does everyone else, so don't mess with me—and that's a union rule."

"That's a fuckin' union rule, then fuck the union rule," Dictado spit as though out of control. He shot open the door and ran into Bob San Pablo, a cannery foreman. Holding San Pablo by the biceps, Dictado drove him back a pace while yelling at Gene in dialect.

San Pablo pushed past Dictado. He rubbed his face and waved a hand in the air as if trying to dislodge the odor. "Did you understand what he said?"

Gene shook his head.

"He said, 'motherfucker, I'll get rid of you.'"

Gene steadied his hands on top of the desk. "What the hell can I say? There're so many threats around this community!"

San Pablo waved him off. "Hey, I'm just translating."

"But why does he need to threaten me in front of you?"

"Sending me a message, too."

"We're going to get this shit all the time, until we put them away or put them down. It's a fight—we either win or lose. Those guys threaten someone every day. Every time they lose a big stake they pat their guns or grip their cocks and talk trash. You can handle it, Robert."

Bob pointed a finger at Gene. "I can handle it. But can you?"

For a couple of days Gene mulled over Dictado's words. Why had Dictado threatened him? Had he been paid to say that? Someone had to be behind him, someone with power, not just the restaurant clique. Gene began to long for the armor he'd dreamed of at Glen's.

He jogged to Silme's place to talk, but Silme had no answers. Silme thought it weird that Dictado had acted so arrogant in front of a witness. "To throw you off maybe, to get you looking one way so they can move in from another direction," he suggested. "Dictado can't be operating on his own. Baruso's been really hard to keep track of since the convention—maybe there's a connection."

Word had gotten round that Baruso had stayed in Honolulu to speak with the Philippine Consulate after the resolution passed. There were so many rumors flying that Gene and Silme almost dropped their guard, not out of weariness or triumph, but because now they felt as if they were spinning in a maelstrom.

On Memorial Day, the KDP gathered with friends and family at Seward Park, along the southern end of Lake Washington. Gene was tired, but spending a day away from the ID helped restore his spirits. Montoya was nowhere to be seen in the crowds of people eating hot dogs and hamburgers and drinking beer and soft drinks. At first Gene thought his absence odd, then sinister. Despite having been booted out of KDP headquarters, Montoya usually attended all their parties and functions.

Gene fell asleep seated upright at a picnic table, holding a hot dog that dripped mustard from its bun. He awoke to amused faces across the table. "Gene's working too much overtime," one of his friends said.

"Gene needs to take more time off," Silme offered, sitting with his older daughter wrapped inside his coat. A breeze had come up and several people were pulling on sweatshirts. Gene rubbed his bare arms.

"Gene needs to get married," Gene put in, reaching to touch Ligaya's dark hair.

Later that evening, his skin puckering to goose bumps after a quick dip in the freezing lake, Gene kissed a woman who'd wanted to be held to keep the cold from doubling her up. For a moment he imagined it was Leila in his arms. When the beams from a passing car lit the woman's face, he pulled away abruptly, touched her hand and said good night. Walking across the parking lot, he entered a phone booth and brought a quarter to the slot. "Curry," he told the Vancouver operator and gave her the name of the street. When a drunken male voice answered, he apologized and hung up.

❋

The next day, Monday, brought a new month. It was a bright day, hot for Seattle, and Gene was having a hard time keeping his mind on work. From the dispatch office, he called Ade Domingo, who was helping to organize the program for Philippine National Day to be held later in June in the International District. Ade was writing the text and Gene was arranging the program. Then he gave the phone to Silme. "A couple more things to do, but I'll be out of here by four-fifteen, Mom."

"Do you think that guy'll come in?" Gene asked when Silme hung up the phone.

"Who, Ramil? He said so." Silme yawned.

"What a jerk that guy is. What'd he say he wants?"

"I don't know. He's your guy, isn't he?"

"Meaning what?" Gene asked.

"You got his records—he says he wants to look at his health plan."

"What health plan? Is he even in the union? Shit, I guess he is. What's he doing?"

"Night school. I hear he's going straight."

"Straight to hell. Is Della coming in?"

"Supposed to be here by now." Silme looked up over Gene's shoulder. "Speak of the devil."

Gene turned to see Ramil, Ben Guloy crowding in beside him. He also caught the profile of Boy Pilay in the hallway, looking around nervously. Pilay was a young Filipino who boasted of a gang-related foot wound; his presence bothered Gene deeply. A gray uneasiness spread to his stomach as he noted the paper bag in Ramil's hand, the way Ramil hefted its obvious weight.

"How's it going, Benny?" Silme mumbled. Benny didn't speak, though Silme had once been his tutor. His hands shook noticeably.

"See my records?" Ramil rasped out.

"What records?" Gene asked. He tried to lock eyes with Silme.

"What kinda health care I got?"

"Same as everyone else."

"Got a right to see it."

"Up to you, man." Gene uprooted himself from his chair and moved to the file cabinet, aware that Pilay was still limping around outside the office. He lifted the file in his hand when the bag Ramil was carrying exploded. Gene felt his back break open. Crimson burst in his eyes. He heard Silme cry out as bullets crashed into walls, and then a crunch of footsteps. As he fell to the floor, he began gargling blood. "Andy, take me home. Dad, where are you? Fly me out of here."

❧

Silme

Ramil raises his arms bag bursts into flame huge erupting pistol look out Gene you're hit Ramil turning on me cracking round the room noise breaks my ears punches me three four times I'm down crawl to Gene pounding inside my spine try to pull Gene over blood spreading over his back he's going he's going oh buddy got to get them Ramil Guloy Pilay should've known get outside hallway spinning hold the wall blood pouring inside filling me up.

Help me Jesus help me I'm shot down the stairs on the street must hold myself hold in blood there's bastard Ramil running through doorway I scream he shot me into a terrified face she

115

yells spins around fireman bending down over me seen his face before somewhere moves me inside smell exhaust two other guys siren screams who did it I tell him now he's writing say it again slowly Ra Meal shows me the paper can't see everything turns dark. Wake up to other name Guloy he's got it right must've said it while I was under blackout takes me down again doctor nurses faces peering probing inside me must be drugged deep are the bullets out my own voice so weak looking down into deep woods Carkeek Park like when I was a kid at dawn when living was on hold newspapers from my route all delivered weight off my shoulders ink covering my hands watching early sun pitch into woods dawn striking green leaves moving over bay water igniting nothing before or since this moment thin mist rising sun on shoreline steady through leaves warming my feet my body my face.

My mother's face breaks through light can you write who hurt you son can't hold pen but know them see them Terri's face now who did it Ramil Guloy I nod yes others drag my hand down my leg pistol-point to foot they get it.

Dawn blazes behind my eyes I reach out hands like spreading wings but they're tugged down by human weights Ligaya Kalyaan Terri my family pulling me back circling slowly if only I could dance with them forever light flares up quiet comes down around me.

116

PART II

Two bullets crushed Gene's back, striking his heart, and he lived for perhaps thirty seconds more. The coroner's report listed his death as "instantaneous." The news devastated friends and family in Wapato. Hardly anyone except Andy Pascua understood the risks Gene had been taking in his job as dispatcher, or was able to believe the depth of his political commitment.

The Domingo family rallied to Silme's hospital bedside. Two of his sisters, Vangie and Cindy, arrived at Harborview Medical Center from Arizona and Oakland the same evening he was shot. So many family members gathered that the hospital had to find them an additional room.

Ade Domingo was particularly distressed that, hours after the shootings, Tony Baruso had still not appeared at the hospital. When she finally reached him by phone at his workplace, he asked if Silme had "talked" and then tried to convince her that he was too busy working to come to the hospital. Baffled and infuriated by his question, Ade pleaded with him that Silme and Gene were his "boys"; he must be there. It was this conversation that caused Ade to begin to wonder if Baruso had a part in the killings.

Terri Mast, on the other hand, had suspected Baruso as soon as her mother-in-law told her that Silme had uttered the names "Guloy" and "Ramil" as he was rushed to the hospital. Terri was sure the two men never would have acted without a directive from their boss, Baruso.

When Ade and Terri revealed their mutual suspicious, Ade decided then and there that, if necessary, she and her husband would spend every dollar they owned to unravel the mystery of the shootings.

Ade's resolve was matched by Terri's, who, even as Silme was fighting for his life, determined that she and other leaders in Local 37 would continue to organize. Within a day of Silme's death, she and David Della returned to work at the union hall wearing bulletproof vests.

Silme was operated on three times within twenty-four hours. The doctors removed three of the four slugs lodged in his abdominal cavity but feared any more surgery would further endanger his life. He died the following afternoon from loss of blood and heart failure. Dave Della and Terri insisted that more than dispatching and gambling had caused Silme's and Gene's assassinations. Della had arrived late to the Monday meeting and found Gene's body stretched on the floor of the office. The memory haunted him. Like Della, many people felt deeply connected to this tragedy. And many people stayed close to the Domingos, forming one essential unit; the killers must have known they faced a formidable opponent. Ade Domingo committed her family's savings; they were going all the way. But they had to look beyond the obvious murderers. As she drove her to the Oakland airport, Geline Aliva reminded Cindy that upon his return from the Philippines, Gene had been red-tagged in Honolulu. It seemed obvious that the men who photographed Gene when he met with the KMU in Malolos knew he was going to be there, which suggested earlier surveillance in the States.

Immediately the families had to mix politics with grief for the loss of these two young men, and with rage at the destructive way the Marcoses, Magsaysay, MacArthur, Roxas and every US president from McKinley to Reagan had taken the Philippines by the throat and wrung it dry. While memorials and rosaries were still being arranged, members of the Domingo family assigned themselves specific roles. Through her invaluable experience with the KDP, Cindy knew how to contact lawyers, arrange press conferences, and form broad-based alliances such as the Committee for Justice for Domingo and Viernes.

Cindy also acted as archivist. She possessed the same instincts as Gene when it came to understanding historical precedents and roles—especially when Gene and her brother were the center of that history. Sometimes she was asked to do more than she felt capable of—answering the telephone, arranging for the memorials— and she had to mix politics and religion with community services, exhausting even with preparation. She had to be ready for questions from the most sympathetic to the most probing reporters, and at the same time bring the slain men's message home to their peers.

Newspapers were stacked on the Domingo's dining room table from Monday, the day of the shooting, to Thursday, the day of Gene's memorial. Cindy and her younger sister, Lynn, who were separating and organizing *Seattle Times* and *Post-Intelligencer* articles, clipped this piece by Gil Bailey from the *PI*: "The union had 'tightened up procedures' in which seniority plays a key role, according to Tony Baruso, veteran president of the union. In the past 'kickbacks' had played a role in the job selection process. Baruso said the murders were an attempt to intimidate the union. 'We are not going to be intimidated. If they are going to shoot all of us here, then they can do it,' he said. 'Killing a number of us will not stop the policy of this union.'"

The Domingos scrutinized every quote attributed to Baruso for possible double meanings. "Kickbacks have been known to occur as a means of getting jobs," Baruso said, and threats against union officials had been made. Baruso said his own life had been threatened in telephone calls. Not once had he mentioned a threatening call to Silme, Gene, or anyone else in the union.

A *Times* article by William Gough read: "Last year a new force emerged in the union when young members of the KDP, a political organization opposed to Philippines President Ferdinand Marcos, were elected officers. Both Viernes and Domingo embraced the organization. 'They are not very strong,' Sylvestre Tangalan, president of the Filipino Community of Seattle, said of the KDP. 'They are very few. They tried to overthrow the Filipino organization in the city, but were not successful,' he said."

To have Sylvestre Tagalan quoted concerning Silme was a bitter pill for the Domingo family. Once, at a Filipino Community of Seattle meeting, the Domingo women had attempted to show how East Coast Filipina nurses were being mistreated and how their group could support the nurses' strike. During the meeting Tangalan yelled a lot, Ade remebered, and Baruso became so agitated that afterward he threatened to shoot people. He kept tapping a gun in his coat pocket. Ade told him, "Go ahead and shoot. Are you ready to die? I am. If you kill me, I'll make sure my sons get you." Baruso didn't shoot anybody but he did corner Nemesio Sr.—whom he considered a friend—and told the older man that Ade was the only woman he'd allow to threaten him that way and not shoot. In 1978, when Ade returned from the Phillipines, she was told she no longer held her office in the Filipino Community.

Thinking of that period and the loss of her committee position, Ade remembered another incident when Baruso had become violent. In 1979, when again she was running for office, Baruso had gone on a rampage, waving a gun around. Silme jumped from the top of a van and with another young man, held him on the floor until his fit was over. The police were called, the incident recorded, but nothing came of it. As Ade reviewed her own history within the Filipino Community, she saw a maze of threats and violence.

Gough's article, quoting Baruso, went on: "'Many young Filipinos opposed to Marcos never have been to the Philippines and are unaware of actual conditions in that nation. Nevertheless,' Baruso said, 'Viernes and Domingo were hard-working, honest and progressive trade-union officers. They were carrying out the union's

121

policy and my policy in instituting fair dispatch procedures for work at the Alaska canneries.'"

❋

Streets were cordoned off to and from the entrance to Local 37. At first the night was stormy but grew quieter as at least three hundred people, according to Wayne Jacobi, covering the event in the Post-Intelligencer, marched from the square in front of the drop-in center in a circular route through the International District to the union hall. People came forward to speak for Gene at both ends of the route, symbolically showing how his life had epitomized the good that was evident in those several blocks. Cindy had met Gene's sister Barbara before, as well as his mother and brothers, Gene having taken her to Wapato on two occasions. The Viernes family's tears were so wrenching that Cindy could hardly express her own loss. It was as though Gene's death had pulled a vital muscle out of them all. She and Andy Pascua stood among the mix of people, holding onto one another tightly. Andy tried to understand the fate that had taken his friend. It was difficult for him not to think that Gene was still there, talking to some young woman in the crowd.

Andy gripped the microphone at the platform. "The reason they had to shoot Gene was that they couldn't change him. He was totally dedicated, totally uncorruptible. Gene was a multifaceted person who never ceased to amaze us with his ability and dedication. Gene was strong, not just physically, but mentally tough. It was natural he should evolve into a leader. Labor organizers have to be translators; people work for different reasons and the leader has to take their needs and translate them into values they understand, then send them back. You have to be able to put yourself aside and that can be hard. A lot of people who get into the movement just disappear. But to be able to do that work and still have clear motives is a great gift. And Gene had that gift more than anybody I ever met.

"He gave up a great deal. He never married, he wasn't wealthy and he had very little time to spend with his family. He wasn't selfish but I think he was weathier than all of us."

Dave Della spoke next for the rank and file of Local 37. He called for the murders to release a "floodgate of outrage and a pledge to redouble our efforts to complete the work that Gene and Silme started." It was the first time this theme was sounded; by the time of Silme's rosary and memorial, it would gain high definition. In three short nights the phrase "turn anguish into anger" became a rallying cry.

Baruso spoke of his basic agreement with Silme and Gene and pledged that the union would continue the reform movement in which Silme and Gene "had played a strong role. Maybe somebody is going to shoot me in the head, too," he said. "But we will not be stifled or changed. We are not going to give up our values. With the help of all unions, we are here to stay and we will not be undermined by those who know how to pull a trigger." Terri's and Cindy's eyes widened with disbelief. Squeezing Cindy's shoulder, Terri whispered loud enough that two others standing in front of them turned to shake their heads. "Shot in the head? They weren't shot in the head. Baruso wants to be shot in the head, I'll volunteer."

As Cindy consoled her friend, she looked around anxiously, aware that she too had fallen into everyone's growing fear. She noticed an overweight man bearing down upon Ade, and nudged Terri. His words were muffled by the layer of people wedged between them but she and Terri heard, "—use the Community Center for Silme's memorial."

Then Ade was screaming in English and Tagalog. "You got the guts to invite us, after you threw me out? You redbaited us! We are the community! How do we know you aren't behind it?" She tried to swing at the man but someone held her back, and the man maneuvered away, red-faced.

❧

Silme's memorial moved in three stages, beginning at the Filipino Community Hall with a difficult ordeal of mixed ritual: lodge, nationalism, union, the open casket exposing his bloated body and head, the Dimas Alang lodge cap held on by hairpins. On the casket stood a glass of whiskey and as they passed the coffin, weeping, several people paused to drink with Silme.

Silme and Terri's two girls found clear passage through their grief by becoming absorbed in the ritual. They liked dressing up for their dad, Ligaya exchanging handshakes with friends and family. By now she at least understood that her father was dead. She believed he was in heaven. Cindy and Terri envied the child her belief and had to acknowledge that if anyone could find a heaven, it would be Silme. He might charm his way in, or, barring that, sue, if angels discriminated.

The following day after burying Gene in Wapato mourners drove all the way to Seattle to attend Silme's funeral at the St. James cathedral. The June light was diffused by tall, stained glass windows. Cindy longed for the dizzying crush of Mass to push her down with Silme, to be momentarily inside with him. If she realized rebirth, recognized it naturally, she could assure it for her brother. Along with so many other Catholics in the movement, technically she had fallen away from the church.

Calvary Cemetery was tougher going, interment more final than the funeral. As strong as Ade had been, now she sagged in her children's arms. The weeping here was as fundamental as their grief for the homeland, confounded by stone crosses, the absolute proof of mortality. Many left the cemetery needing to be restored by the march and the union hall singing still to come.

❖

Five hundred people spilled out of the union hall onto the street. Hanging above the mourners, flowered wreaths and the ensemble playing soft music was an unembellished black-on-white sign: TURN ANGUISH INTO ANGER. Silme's memorial coincided with the date they had selected for Filipino National Day, the celebration Ade, Gene, and Silme had been working on when the two men were shot. Those gathered sang a traditional mourning song, and then the speakers came forward.

"The murders of Silme and Gene were so cold-blooded, they were an attack on this organization," George Martin, an ILWU vice president, said. "Those killers who were behind this think we will roll over and play dead. It will not happen."

Leni Marin of the KDP reminded the crowd of their deceased friends' opposition to Marcos, their commitment to "revolutionary changes."

Velma Fernandez, one of Ade's friends, spoke fondly of Silme's efforts to organize the Filipino community, "sometimes opening wounds between generations. Some ideas may be too young, but like a plant from a seed, they may grow," she said. "Later on the plants may bear the fruits of love and order."

Nemesio Sr. got up bravely, aided by his cane. He thanked those at the service for the comfort they had brought his family. Then all present sang the old Wobbly song, "Solidarity Forever": *When the union's inspiration through the worker's blood shall run, there can*

124

be no power greater anywhere beneath the sun.

Throughout the memorial, Terri stood beside Cindy and Shari Woo, their everpresent sisterhood offering her solace. Tears flowing, she placed her arms around her friends as they sang an old Filipino immigration song.

> While still across the ocean,
>   I heard about the U.S.A.,
> So thrilled by wild imagination
>   I left home through Manila Bay.
>
> Then on the way I thought and wondered
>   Alone what would the future be?
> I gambled parental care and love
>   In search for human liberty.
>
> But beautiful bright pictures painted
>   Were just half of the whole story ...
> Reflections of great wealth and power
>   In the land of slavery.
>
> Minorities in shanty towns, slums ...
>   Disgraceful spots for all to see
> In the enviable Garden of Eden
>   Land of affluence and poverty.

Terri and Cindy had taken no chances with the ultimate meaning of Silme's memorial. After singing the immigrant song and "Solidarity Forever," the crowd ended the memorial with "The Internationale." "It was Silme's favorite," Cindy told *PI* reporter Gil Bailey.

❊

The next day the press got busy focusing upon the murders. The June 5, 1981, *Seattle PI* editorialized: "... the local and federal authorities also have an obligation—to press their investigation in the motives for the crimes ... to determine if corruption still exists in the union and if so, to prosecute the wrongdoers."

The *Seattle Times* offered this opinion: "Union Killings are More than 'Routine' Homicides ... the investigation into the deaths should include a probe—by the FBI if necessary—of past and present job-dispatching practices.

"Insistence must be made by the union, the canneries, the Filipino community, and appropriate federal agencies that clear-cut job-dispatching regulations exist—ones that can bring quick enforcement against any irregularities."

The *Times* editorial offered hope that the issue was not being slanted from the start against unions. Members of Local 37 agreed that the FBI might break precedent by investigating the canneries' practices rather than their usual approach of harrassing the ILWU about its politics.

On the day of the arraignment, the courthouse was packed. People jammed the corridors. Spokespeople informed the city about the recent formation of the Committee for Justice for Domingo and Viernes, an ad hoc group composed of family and community members. The CJVD soon received endorsement as a legitimate community enterprise from, among other organizations, the Church Council of Greater Seattle. The Church Council endorsement turned out to be a useful means of unifying sympathetic groups. From the outset the murders pulled at peoples' minds and consciences as well as hearts, because the killing of these young men said, "it can happen here."

The Committee for Justice insisted that Tony Baruso head the list of community members who signed their declaration. Much less gratuitous than Tony's support were the endorsements of Seattle City Council members Dolores Sibonga, Norman Rice, and Michael Hildt, and every Filipino organization in the city.

At the arraignment, Bob Santos stood in the hallway of the courthouse and reminded the gathering that while the Filipino community had been cowed by violence, that was in the past. "We've let it go on without challenging it, but no more. We are pledged to bring this senseless violence to a halt."

Arrested for the murder, Jimmy Ramil and Ben Guloy pleaded not guilty. Because every possible interpretation of the crime indicated powerful enemies, the Committee for Justice knew it would need the strongest charge available: in this case, aggravated murder. Prosecution lawyers would need to prove there had been a conspiracy to assassinate Silme and Gene, a difficult task to achieve in a criminal case. Finding Guloy and Ramil guilty might be easy, but linking them to those who pulled their strings might be impossible.

A solid legal team formed behind the Committee within three

days of the murders. Michael Withey, a friend of the Domingos who had been Local 37's attorney from the time of Silme and Gene's elections, volunteered immediately. Many on the Committee for Justice agreed with Withey that the hit men were only "the lowest branches" of a tree that would eventually reveal the entire conspiracy, if only they could see around the killers. Committee and Local 37 people met daily to discuss the ways in which the conspiracy might have worked. On butcher paper in Michael's office, Nemesio Jr. drew three interesting circles representing possible threats to the murdered men: one was Marcos, another the canneries because of the lawsuits, and the third was Baruso and the Tulisan. They knew from the state that dispatch alone was not enough motive for murder: as president, Tony Baruso had the constitutional right to dispatch over Gene's head, should he choose to do so. Silme and Gene being elected could not have motivated Baruso this early, because he did not stand to lose his job to them for two or three years. He was well off; his gambling proceeds amounted only to about $2,000—not enough for a motive. Still, Baruso was the only one whose interests seemed to intersect all three of the circles of threat, especially with regard to his loyalty, both personally and politically, to Marcos. And Marcos had a track record for assassination. So the word went out, "Watch Baruso." Report back his every response, to the arrests of Guloy and Ramil, for example; his expressions, his attitudes, because eventually he will lead us to an understanding of the conspiracy.

Money for the case was difficult to come by. As John Caughlan, another of the families' legal advisors, put it, "Virtually all the legal work over the years was pro bono. For a short time I think we were compensated at the rate of about $10 per hour for the actual legal time spent. That dried up relatively quickly. A few fundraisers brought in a little money ... but for the most part it was financed right out of people's pockets. The Viernes family contributed all of their insurance money and more to this case. And the Domingo family contributed almost everything they had."

Being found guilty of aggravated murder would mean either the death penalty or mandatory life imprisonment, without hope of parole. The first hurdle the Committee for Justice had to jump concerned the death penalty, which had recently been reinstated as a legal means of punishment in the state of Washington. The Committee feared the case might become a *cause celebre* for the death penalty if the prosecution chose that option. People who might naturally have supported the CJDV's case—churches, minorities, those with legal objections—might have been forced to abandon their support. When the CJDV met with their growing legal team, they decided they did not want death as a penalty and were able to persuade the prosecution in favor of their choice.

The Domingo family particularly was against the death penalty; they wanted to find the defendants guilty of aggravated murder and sentence them to life without parole. It was a perfect strategy: the families sincerely meant their charge and hoped that others would be named as the case rolled along, which would practically guarantee the charge of conspiracy. By going out of their way to ask the prosecutor to avoid the death penalty, they avoided any slander that they longed for blood revenge.

Meanwhile Local 37 was running a finely drawn course of its own. Terri had so much to do, she was left with little idle time in which to grieve, the result being that daily she became a more accomplished leader. At first she resisted an FBI investigation on the basis of old anxieties, their wiretapping of Harry Bridges in the 1950s being a major point. But if the union resisted investigation, they would pass up the opportunity to probe unsavory cannery practices, such as harrassment of workers, racism, and involvement in interstate gambling—charges the union had already made stick against cannery owners.

Then Terri thought, why not try to mold the FBI? If, in a news conference, the union explained why they didn't trust the FBI, perhaps the federal organization would be put on the defensive. The FBI might actually work to the union's advantage. Such a tactic was worth the risk, especially if they could get the FBI to read the Alaska Cannery Workers' Association's lawsuit as a motive for the hiring of company hit men.

Cindy pulled the following item from the June 14 *Seattle Times*: Investigation, Not Intimidation.

In response to your editorial (June 3) we agree that there must be a thorough investigation of these criminals who caused the death of our brothers, Gene Viernes and Silme Domingo. Although two suspects are now in custody, we believe that others may be responsible for this vicious attack. They also must be brought to justice.

... an FBI investigation of the internal affairs of the union ... treats the victim as the suspect. The public can rest assured democratic dispatch of cannery workers to Alaska will be performed in the manner prescribed by union officers, including Gene Viernes and Silme Domingo.

... Rather than investigating the union, law enforcement should aggressively pursue any leads to establish who was responsible for this attack on the union.

—Constantine "Tony" Baruso, President, Local 37, ILWU

Tony signed the letter, but behind his signature was the mind of the reform slate, and their intention to maintain an offensive stance. Nevertheless, when Terri and Mike tried to work with the FBI, principally to discover Baruso's connection to the crimes, they were at first encouraged, and ultimately frustrated. They were helped by an agent named Lee Zavala, honest and hard-working, who indicated that he wanted to go to the grand jury to charge Baruso when he'd learned that a cannery employee had overheard Baruso bragging about the size of the bullet holes in Silme and Gene. Weeks went by, and Terri and Mike heard nothing; finally they called the FBI, only to learn that Zavala no longer worked for the agency, having taken a job as head of security for Sealand. They were told their investigation was hampered by the fact that a certain document was missing from Zavala's file. Mike Withey met Zavala for lunch, and when the ex-agent was informed of the "missing" document, he left the table, walked straight to his former office, opened the files. There was the document, which he then copied, putting the original back into the file.

Still, when Mike and Terri talked with Gene Anderson, the US Attorney, and George Fisher of the FBI about arresting Baruso, they were told that granting Baruso immunity might be the best strategy. Mike and Terri vehemently disagreed; they could not understand the others' reasoning, which was that it would be easier "to get Dictado" if Baruso were free to talk. But the Committee never doubted they could convict Dictado. It seemed a poor strategy, to avoid the higher branch to swat a lower one. Yet Baruso avoided arrest.

❋

Terri met Cindy for lunch at the Elliott Bay Cafe and told her she was learning to stand up to Baruso. "I was at a meeting with him the other night. You know how he's always telling people to shut up? I'd never taken charge before, but I jumped up and said, 'Don't shut anyone up! You're full of shit. Don't claim anything for Silme and Gene, either. You're not for us and you know it.'" She laughed. "Pretty brave, huh? I don't know if I told you—we've been hassled by gang members driving past when we come out of meetings, screaming at us. And last night I nearly passed out—Dictado came right up to the room where we were meeting to give us hell! About the only time I was glad Baruso was there. We came down from meetings, all of us wearing our vests, and there were gang members lining the walls, calling us 'Mao Maos.' I have second thoughts every time I turn my car key."

"Letelier," Cindy said, referring to Orlando Letelier, a Chilean leader of the opposition who was murdered in Washington, DC, by Pinochet's agents on September 21, 1976.

But Terri's latest nightmare was closer to home: either Silme had failed to sign the union's life insurance policy or, his name had been left off by error. Cindy was shocked but Terri tried to reassure her—and herself—by telling her that John Caughlan was handling the matter by bringing a suit against the company. Forgetting to sign the policy—which, ironically, Silme had only recently drawn up for all union officers—seemed a minor flaw when held against his foresight of anticipating the need for insurance.

Cindy asked Terri how their watch on Baruso was going.

"He doesn't know what to do. One minute he's his old bastard self, the next he's nervously assuring us of his support, then he's off somewhere trying to 'find something on us.' Ever since we started calling his act, he's stepped up the pressure. We were at a meeting with the International and he says, 'I know what you guys were doing last night,' and 'I know where you were, you guys were having a meeting,' making all these accusations. Then in the middle of the meeting he makes a phone call outside and comes back with more ammunition against us, implying we're working with the Communist Party, any kind of nonsense. He has to be talking to someone because whenever he leaves, he returns with new stuff. We've traced some numbers he's been calling since the murders, but we don't know agents. He might work through the CIA but what would that mean?"

Perplexed, Cindy shook her head.

Terri described to Cindy the way she and Mike Withey had been frustrated in their attempt to have Baruso arrested; the US Attorney's suggestion that offering him immunity was the best strategy. "Their theory is he'll be free to testify, to grant names. They say they want him to sweat, have someone else name him. But we see an implication that someone, maybe the State Department, is saying, 'Lay off Baruso.'"

Cindy wanted more news of the union.

"Your sister, Lynn, goes in as secretary-treasurer. Nobody's going to oppose that—she's Silme's sister and she's KDP. Next move is to get our people in the dispatching spot. We're gonna put together a team, Dave Della, maybe two others. That way we'll feel less targeted than if we worked alone. Next we get Baruso out of there, soon as we have the votes for no-confidence. Then a recall." Terri paused, breathing deeply. "Is the family holding any more rosary nights? They're killing me."

Cindy touched her friend's hand. "Tonight's the ninth one, a big feast."

Terri pushed her blueberry cheesecake in Cindy's direction.

Ramil's and Guloy's attorneys wanted a change of venue. They protested the courtroom presence of tape recorders and television cameras showing the two men, chained, being led into the room, arguably a heavy image for the jury. Their request was denied.

King County provided Joanne Maida as Deputy Prosecutor, a choice that pleased the victims' families. From the start, Maida, a Japanese American, seemed willing to listen sympathetically to the families' lawyers' strategies. She immediately rose against the defense's argument concerning the new charge, pointing out that the double killing met the definition of aggravated murder because a single act resulted in the death of both victims.

The next day the *Seattle Times* printed an article by Dick Clever entitled, "Filipinos: A Family Deeply Split." Cindy read parts of it to Lynn, who was making coffee in the Domingo kitchen. "The writer calls Dimas Alang 'a fraternal organization with roots in the turn-of-the-century Philippines ... a protective society begun under Spanish rule ... transplanted to the US with the first immigrants ... Silme Domingo had long criticized the organization as a bastion of conservatism.'"

"He would have said worse than that," Lynn called out.

"He says Silme joined to establish 'better rapport' with old-timers ... goes on to mention Tulisan members hanging out at the King Street lodge."

"Coffee's ready—"

"Listen to this," Cindy quoted, "'Domingo and his family were involved with members of the KDP in a bitter fight to gain control of the Filipino Community Council ... the KDP has been labeled communist by both moderate and more conservative elements of the Filipino community ... however, Leni Marin, a Seattle KDP leader, says it is an oversimplification to color the group as communist-oriented.'"

Lynn pushed aside piles of newspapers on the dining room table to deliver Cindy's coffee. "Get to the point."

"It's here. How Dad abstained in the 1978 election ... 'That gave Tony Baruso ... the power to choose the new secretary-treasurer. He chose someone other than Silme.'"

"That's it?"

"No—here's you: 'Silme and Gene had become revolutionaries,'" said Silme's sister, Lynn. "'They were attacking the root causes of oppresion.'"

"All right!" Lynn lifted the article, her face glowing with a hint of Silme's mischievous expression. Cindy recalled an occasion when their parents, angry with something a ten-year-old Silme had done, chased him through the house. Silme ran into the kitchen, Ade and Nemesio on his heels. They ran around one side of the table while Silme dipped under it and ran out the back door, a big grin on his face. Their parents bumped heads trying to catch him, then yelled at each other. Now that was a family "deeply split," the sisters agreed in reminiscence, and laughed.

❉

Three nights later Mike Withey called the Domingos to tell them that Tony Baruso had been arrested in his home on two counts of murder and booked into the King County jail. Earlier someone from the police department called Withey to ask him if Baruso's first name was Constantine. Mike said it was and asked what they had: The policeman couldn't say, but the following day Mike learned that the police had what appeared to be the murder weapon, a .45 caliber Mac 10 automatic pistol—registered to Baruso, and sitting in a police locker for ten days. When the weapon was placed before him at the police station, Baruso said, "What is this?" the police responded. "You've never seen it? It belongs to you." Tony told the police it had been stolen from his car, but he'd never reported it. The crucial fact of this piece of evidence was that Tony had reported two other stolen weapons to his insurance agent. For this particular weapon, which was quite expensive, he'd never bothered to process a claim.

Baruso's attorney wanted the police to arrest the man who'd led them to the pistol. He was a pensioner, digging in garbage cans for a "supplementary income." The garbage cans were near Lincoln Park, close to Tony Dictado's place.

After police recovered the murder weapon and traced its ownership, Baruso was released. No charges were filed against him. It shocked the victims' families to have him in their grasp and then lose him so easily, once again suggesting he had stronger connections than the union and Boeing.

❈

Since the families' attorneys had no plans to call her as a witness, Cindy was able to watch the whole trial. This allowed her the freedom to think and plan their future strategy, taking notes while one after another of the defense witnesses seemed bent on hanging either themselves or their friends.

Assistant Prosecutor Joanne Maida built a case for the jury. She linked the murders to gambling, hoping the strategy would reveal a conspiracy. Maida implicated Tony Baruso, asserting that he was deeply disappointed when new union policies guaranteed a denial of his share of the gambling proceeds, and that Jimmy Ramil and Ben Guloy worked for him in the Tulisan. Maida told jurors that Ramil and Guloy "acted on the orders of others."

Maida argued that the old guard of Local 37 cooperated with the Tulisan by dispatching their people to various canneries to make certain that gambling operations continued. Big money was involved, with pots reaching $1,000 in some games. The reform movement was threatening gambling operations. "Under the new rules," she stated, "members of Tulisan had no seniority. Most of them were at the third preference level, so they were unable to get up to Alaska to enforce the operation."

Maida went on to say that on May 26, Dictado told Viernes to dispatch "two of his boys" to Dillingham, even though they did not have seniority. When Gene refused, Dictado threatened him in a Filipino dialect Gene did not understand: "Motherfucker, I'll get rid of you."

Robert San Pablo was key to this testimony and, though he eventually testified against the Tulisan, Terri and Mike Withey were never sure they trusted him. They came close to hearing his evidence when—late in June—they'd been asked to fly to the Peter Pan plant in Dillingham to hear a grievance. Tony Baruso had insisted that he fly with them. When they walked into the office of the Dillingham plant, there sat Percival Draculan, who had not been first preference, the plant owner, and Robert San Pablo, the foreman.

When Mike and Terri left the meeting, San Pablo cornered Mike and asked him where he was staying. Mike was scared; he and Terri still wore their bullet-proof vests. Mike, feeling particularly vulnerable, stayed in the Filipino barracks. Baruso overheard San Pablo inquire, and subsequently followed Mike closely, which was okay with him, because he was keeping an eye on Baruso. Suddenly they saw Boyse Campo coming from the office, saying there was an urgent call for Boy Pilay. Terri and Mike were shocked—both of these men were Tulisan; neither was supposed to be dispatched, and Boy was a murder suspect. Terri followed Boyse and tried to overhear Pilay's phone conversation; Baruso insisted that they all three had to leave at once to catch a plane for the Bumblebee plant.

Within days after Baruso, Terri, and Mike flew away, San Pablo came to the plant owner with the information that he'd received a letter from Baruso saying, "I couldn't talk to you with those Mao-Maos around," reminding San Pablo that he owed him $1,500 in gambling cuts. Boy Pilay delivered the letter, bragging that Baruso had paid hit men $5,000 to kill Gene and Silme. The plant owner sent San Pablo to the Dillingham Police. They took his deposition and informed the Seattle Police, who eventually delivered him to the trial. San Pablo's deposition revealed that Tony Dictado and Baruso held a private meeting two days before the shootings, and that the night before, Ramil had told San Pablo, "Tony (Dictado) is going to get Viernes tomorrow."

James Grubb, Ramil's lawyer, saw his client differently from the prosecution. Jimmy Ramil was married, taking a welding course until his arrest, and was a dealer in a place that did, in fact, have gambling. He worked for Charles Penor who operated a club on King Street, evidently ignored by the police. The club wasn't a big-time gambling operation. "It is called the Oldtimer's Club and low-stakes domino games are played there," Grubb said.

Anthony Meyers, attorney for Ben Guloy, made the same case as Grubb, but provided as much credibility for the victims as for his client. Once more he implicated Dictado and Baruso. It seemed as if Ramil's and Guloy's attorneys thought they had a chance to get their clients off by aiming at Baruso and Dictado; the prosecution's goal was to nail all four of them.

Meyers told the jurors there was no evidence that Guloy and Ramil belonged to the Tulisan or had a motive for the murders. Guloy knew Silme and was at the union office that day to "pay him back money he owed him." Guloy's alibi was that he spent the afternoon at a club and park in the ID and did not return to the union hall.

According to Meyers, a high school student and a bus driver would testify that only one man was seen fleeing the scene after shots rang out. The student evidently saw a Filipino male wearing a shiny black jacket with white cuffs run from the hall and get into a parked car. "The getaway car was a dead match to the car Dictado drives—a black TransAm with an eagle on the hood," Meyers said. Meyers continued to explain how, four weeks later, the murder weapon showed up in a trash can in Lincoln Park, near Dictado's home. The can had been emptied regularly before the gun was discovered so it could not have been in there long. Meyers added, "Whoever dumped the weapon was not Ramil or Guloy because they were in jail at the time. It was Tony Dictado."

The next day Tony Dictado turned up in court with his alibi: he had been gambling at the time of the murders; witnesses would back this up. Dictado testified just hours after police arrested him. Maida said she had Dictado picked up on a material witness warrant because she "expected to have difficulty producing him at trial."

Grubb, Ramil's attorney, had told Maida of Dictado's whereabouts and was angry with her tactic. "I think it is bad faith for Ms. Maida to take my information and use it as a basis for the arrest," he complained.

This remark prompted Meyers to say that Grubb seemed to be wearing two hats at the trial. "He is representing a defendant in this case, and it seems as though he is also trying to represent Mr. Dictado."

The apparent conflict between Guloy's and Ramil's lawyers prompted this remark from John Stamets' coverage of the case for the *Seattle Sun*: "In establishing that some sort of conspiracy did take place, the prosecution is getting a big boost from defense attorneys Tony Meyers and James Grubb."

Patricia Wilson, the high school witness, was fairly certain the man she'd seen running from the scene was neither Ramil nor Guloy. But nothing she said hurt the prosecution's case because it was possible that three people were involved—including Pilay, maybe four—all running in different directions.

"This guy was coming out of the building and fell to the ground," she said, and described a second man coming out of the union hall, "a little bit after the other guy fell." He hurried to a black TransAm

135

parked nearby, got in, and sped up Main Street, she said adding that the man was Filipino, wearing white pants, a black karate-type jacket, and low, flat shoes. "He was big like him," Wilson said, motioning to Dictado, "but his hair and mustache were different." She was positive the man wasn't Ramil or Guloy, either.

Dictado admitted he owned a TransAm like the one described but said he was at the Oldtimer's Club on the day of the shootings. He insisted that Ramil and Guloy were there with him. Perhaps Dictado knew that all three had to get off, or their link to Baruso would be obvious. Dictado denied that Ramil and Guloy belonged to the Tulisan, which was only a group of "four close friends, not a gang."

The next day Baruso's co-worker at Boeing testified that Tony had come to him in December wanting to buy a Mac 10 .45 semi-automatic. The man referred him to a gun dealer but the dealer was out of stock, so he sold Tony his own gun, which was "like new."

Rudy Schmitz, the elderly fellow who'd found the gun, testified that he was in the habit of searching garbage cans to augment his income.

The prosecution was counting on an elderly witness to identify the killers. Earlier in the afternoon of the murders, Benny Caluya had talked to Silme. While in court he decided he'd seen "no one." Maida reminded him that the day before he'd said that he had seen two young guys in the union hallway, and he'd admitted to flunking a polygraph test when he told one policeman he didn't see anyone. Caluya blamed the polygraph results on poor procedures. "They keep me there and they keep me there and I was so hungry I just want to go home."

Maida asked if he'd changed his testimony out of fear, which he denied. The next day's newspapers implied that Caluya's testimony was a setback but, watching the jurors' faces, Cindy was sure they believed the man had been threatened.

The prosecution's prize witness came forward on August 26. Robert San Pablo, the foreman at the Dillingham plant, part of the reform slate, was determined to stamp the rackets out of the union. He told the jury he had stayed out of Seattle earlier that summer because his life had been threatened shortly after the murders. He was being held in a secret location for his own protection, as the prosecution was also sure he'd be "taken care of" if anyone on the other side knew what he was going to testify.

Immediately before the threat on his life, he'd received two extortion letters in Dillingham: one from Baruso, the other from Dictado. The letters demanded $1,500 apiece, the amount Baruso and Dictado figured was due them from illegal gambling games, what they'd received from previous cannery foremen. Someone had slipped the first letter into San Pablo's pocket when a work crew arrived at the cannery on June 15. The letter, signed by Dictado, asked him to "kindly lend $1500. I need it for the hospital bill." The second letter, dated July 2, was from Baruso and closed with, "One more thing—I'm supposed to have money from you. Why don't you just mail it to me at my home?"

"Did one of Dictado's boys come to Dillingham while you were there?" Maida asked him.

"Yes. Boy Pilay."

"Did Pilay threaten you?"

"Yes. I was supposed to give him money or, 'he's gonna shoot me. He's gonna kill me. And one more thing, he's gonna blow up my car.'"

At that point in the proceedings, Pilay had been missing for two days. Some feared he had been killed to keep him from the stand.

❋

The following week proved to be a formidable one for the prosecution. It began with testimony from Jim Miller, a young man who said that about an hour before the shooting, he saw Dictado, Guloy, and a third man "casing" the area around the union hall in a black Pontiac TransAm with an eagle decal on the hood. Miller testified that later, minutes after the arrival of emergency fire crews at the union hall, he spotted the car speed away with only the driver. Miller was a commercial fisherman who in the off-season built cabinets at a Pioneer Square wood shop. He hadn't realized the significance of what he'd seen until he read a news account describing the car and its relevance to the case.

When he first saw the car, the driver was alone. "I was a little frightened looking at him," he said. "He had hard features, muscular. He looked like a powerful person." Miller saw the car again between three and three-thirty in the afternoon as he was sitting on the steps of his shop taking a break. There were two passengers in the car, "driving very slowly. Everyone in the car was looking around. I commented to my friend, 'It looks like they're casing the place.'"

Five or ten minutes later, Miller said he saw the three drive by again slowly. At around four-thirty he observed the car a fourth time. "The car came through the intersection at a rapid speed and headed out of sight. This time the driver was alone."

The previous week the police had shown Miller a montage including photos of Dictado and both defendants. Miller had pointed to Dictado as the man who most resembled the driver of the car, but he changed his mind in court. He told the jurors he now believed Guloy was the driver. It mattered little that Miller had doubts about exactly who was driving. His was the first testimony linking Ramil, Guloy, and Dictado together—at the same time, at the same place.

❋

The next day a man who "used to run with the gang" identified Ramil and Guloy as "hard core members" of Tulisan. Angel Doniego had been one of the founding members of KDP. A Vietnam vet, he suffered from post-combat stress and alcoholism, and had dropped out of the KDP from 1978 to 1980 and drifted into the Tulisan.

"They are soldiers," Angel told the jury. "They're the ones who carry out the orders of the leader."

Doniego, who had rejoined the union and reform movement, was done with Tulisan and considered Guloy an enemy. Doniego had been involved in gambling in Alaska and connected to gambling clubs protected by the Tulisan in the ID. He identified Dictado as the leader of Tulisan.

Doniego came under heavy cross-examination from both defense attorneys, but he held up well. People who knew Angel—Terri, in particular—saw him as one of the most courageous witnesses. He could be killed for identifying Dictado, but he had loved Silme, with whom he had roomed for a time. And after delivering his testimony, he planned to move far from Seattle.

The next day Cindy archived a letter responding to the article describing Seattle Filipinos as a family "deeply split." Greg Castilla thanked the *Times* for having the decency to address the issue, which so often had been presented in terms of controversy.

"It is true that Seattle's Filipino community is split. It cannot avoid being so because within the 'family' are two opposed value systems ... those whose idea of service is limited to sponsoring luaus, holding beauty contests, conducting vocational classes ... and those whose commitment confronts issues like immigration problems, unfair union practices ... oppression and racism and social injustice both here and in the homeland. Such a diversity naturally leads to division.

This division ... is healthy. While it shows that there are people in the community who do not want to learn and change, there are others who have already learned and want change. Handled properly, such a polarization will eventually lead to a deeper Filipino unity."

❦

Tony Baruso took the stand and pleaded the Fifth Amendment one hundred nine times. After thirty-seven minutes of questioning, he told the jury only his height, five feet six inches, and his weight, one hundred forty-two pounds.

"Did you kill Mr. Gene Viernes?" A prosecution lawyer asked.

"I refuse to answer on the grounds of self-incrimination."

"Did you kill Mr. Silme Domingo?"

"I also refuse to answer that question on the grounds of self-incrimination."

Baruso's attorney, Tony Savage, seated beside him, tapped Baruso's forearm every time he wanted him to take the Fifth.

Maida asked, "Are you a member of Local 37?"

Savage's hand pressed Baruso's arm. "I refuse to answer on the grounds of self-incrimination."

Baruso acknowledged that he was born in the Philippines and for the past twenty-five years had worked for Boeing. He pleaded the Fifth again when Maida brought up the murder weapon, refusing to tell if he had purchased the gun, why, and if he had denied telling police it was his.

Maida placed the semi-automatic pistol in front of him. She asked if this were the gun he had purchased in December. Savage touched Baruso's forearm.

Baruso also refused to reveal if he had reported the gun stolen, if he had any dealings with Tony Dictado or dispatched any of Dictado's followers to Alaska in violation of new dispatching procedures, and if he had tried to extort $1,500 from Robert San Pablo.

Frank Urpman, the firefighter who came to Silme's aid, testified that Silme had repeated Ramil's and Guloy's names three times. Urpman said he was at his fire station when he heard a man crying for help on the street outside the nearby union hall. He found the man sitting on the ground, bracing himself with his hands. "I asked him what happened. He said he'd been shot. I said, 'Were you robbed?' He said, 'No, I think they're still inside the building.'" Urpman said there were five or six bullet holes in Silme's abdomen, and that another firefighter asked him, "Do you know who shot you?"

At first Urpman didn't write down the names, but asked Silme again, seconds later, who had shot him. "He said the same names, Jim Ramil and Ben Guloy. This time I started writing it down." The defense tried to show that Urpman had written "Rammo" rather than Ramil. He conceded that he had been confused about whether Silme was pronouncing the name "Ram-ee-o" or "Ram-eel" but said he became convinced the name was Ramil.

❅

On August 31, 1981, Rick Anderson, a *Seattle Times* columnist, wrote a piece about a young man from the Philippines, who, after falling in with street toughs, quickly became a thief and hoodlum. Teodorico Domingues, known as Boy Pilay, had first become involved in crime because he heard gunfire in the street next to his car, saw men running—one of them bleeding from bullet wounds—and was told to follow them. He stayed the night with these toughs, though he missed out on making a blood oath with them over a broken whiskey bottle because he'd passed out on the floor. When he awoke, cops were arresting everyone in the room.

Anderson followed a tangled web of extortion, murder, and gambling in which Boy Pilay was always peripherally involved. Five years later, it came as no surprise to find him on the stand of the Viernes-Domingo murder trial, proudly telling the judge and court that he was a Tulisan member and pulling down his shirt to show off the gang's tattoo.

Anderson concluded, "Boy Pilay somehow seemed to think he finally was running in the right direction." But he failed to mention Pilay's role in the murder trial: It was he who had carried an extortion and murder threat from Tony Dictado to Robert San Pablo.

The trial moved into September. Dictado was arrested and charged with two counts of aggravated murder, a giant step for the prosecution. Nobody was saying Dictado pulled the trigger, but that he arranged the shootings, exactly what was needed to prove murder by conspiracy.

Maida said that shortly before the shootings a "distinctive black Pontiac Trans Am" had been seen slowly circling union headquarters as the vehicle's three occupants cased the union hall. Dictado had been tentatively identified as the driver and was seen standing outside the union office with Boy Pilay a short time later.

Maida concluded by saying that Dictado had threatened to kill San Pablo, that he'd bragged he was responsible for the death of Rudy Nazario earlier that year, and that the prosecution witnesses were therefore being kept in protective custody.

❧

Three months had passed since Silme died. Terri tried to keep busy to fend off depression. She told friends she often dreamed he was right there trying to tell her about how he was organizing where he now resided. She hoped it was somewhere more real than heavenly; he was such a realist, a landscape full of angels would bore him. Her lawyers wanted her to testify and she planned to, though she hated the thought. She told herself that if Silme had the guts to incriminate Boy Pilay as he lay dying, she could take the stand for him.

Mike Withey had planned to use Terri's testimony from the ouset. She'd had to learn the courtroom setup from the newspapers, Cindy, Withey, and the rest of the legal team because, as a potential witness, she was not allowed to attend.

Driving downtown through the muggy September heat, Ade squeezed Terri's arm and told her not to worry, she'd set her up. The prosecution's plan was for both of them to focus on Silme's identification of Boy Pilay. She'd warm the chair, Ade told her. The jurors loved Ade. She was salty and tough, and really wanted to nail the killers. The jurors' smiles told everyone watching that they admired Ade for wanting to settle the score. "I saw Silme point to his leg in the hospital bed," Ade told them. "I asked, 'Do you want to tell me who hurt you? Do you want a pen and paper?' I handed the pen to him. I held the clipboard and he tried to write. He was trying to make a circle but he was so weak."

When Joanne Maida called Terri to the stand, she wanted to know if Silme tried to convey more names from his hospital bed.

"He was holding my hand," Terri responded, "and he kept pulling, he was so insistent, pointing his finger at his leg, making a gun motion. I asked if he was hurt there. He said no." Maida asked if Silme had

141

been acquainted with a young man known as Boy Pilay. "'Pilay,'" she told the jury, "is a Filipino name for cripple."

"Yes," Terri answered, "Silme once told me that Pilay became crippled when a friend shot him in the leg." At that point, Terri knew she could go wherever Maida wanted to take her. She had spoken for her husband and helped reach their goal—one more step toward the men at the top. When she sat back on the wooden bench beside Ade, Ade dug her fingers into Terri's forearm.

On September 11, Boyse Campo testified that Guloy and Ramil were in a gambling club when the murders took place on June 1. Ramil and Guloy were not members of the Tulisan, he asserted, which was really only a group of four friends—Dictado, Danny Lorencio, Boy Pilay, and himself. "It's not a gang, it's like a brotherhood. We just hang around."

Ramil's wife, Josie, told jurors that she and Ramil ate dinner together on the night of the shooting. Ramil went out later to attend a welding class. She claimed not to know that Silme and Gene had been murdered until the next day, when her nine-year-old son called her at work and asked, "Mom, how come everything at home is messed up?" Mrs. Ramil said her landlord then got on the phone to inform her that a police detective had come to the home and arrested her husband.

Silme's father was summoned to the witness stand by the defense. He said he talked with Guloy at the union hall on the morning of June 1. Guloy had come in with Ramil. Nemesio Sr. remembered Guloy asking where Silme was. The older man told him Silme wasn't there and asked Guloy to leave whatever he had with him. Guloy insisted, however, that he must see Silme.

It was hard to imagine the point of such testimony. Many people on the family's side had begun to think that nothing the defense attorneys had brought out was a help to Guloy and Ramil. On the other hand, Terri and Cindy wondered why the prosecution seemed so bent on aiming at gambling alone, forgetting Gene's and Silme's real political work.

After trial one day, Terri was having a drink with Cindy before heading to Ballard to pick up her children. Together they tried to sort out the most bizarre bit of testimony they had heard thus far. A man named Levane Forsythe, who evidently had phoned James Grubb, Guloy's attorney, said he had been across the street when Silme was shot. He claimed he had run to his aid, then back to a phone booth. Someone was on the line, though, so he didn't make the call, and by the time he got back, people told him Silme was already taken care of. He got on a ferry and went home. "It's not like I was abandonin' the guy, y'know what I mean? I'm not the kind of guy who likes to get involved in this type of thing—"

Forsythe, eyes red behind hornrimmed glasses, had taken the stand in green polyester slacks and a checked sport coat. He said that Silme had told him he "did not know" who shot him. The Domingo family was stunned.

Then, after the noon break, Joanne Maida strode in, glancing at the family bench.

"Isn't it true," she asked Levane Forsythe, "that you told a jury under oath in 1978 that you were the secret courier who delivered the Mormon will, that is, the infamous 'Howard Hughes Mormon Will,' to Melvin Dummar, a service station operator in the Utah desert?"

Forsythe stayed calm. "Well, as a matter of fact I was the person who delivered it to Dummar. Interesting you should mention that. I worked off and on for Howard Hughes for thirty years. I'm still a close friend of his secretary."

"And didn't you pop up as a surprise witness in the middle of that trial to make those claims?"

"Well, I don't know about 'pop up,'" Forsythe said. "And I was telling the truth when I said them."

Maida told the court that the jury in that trial had determined the incident involving the will to be a hoax perpetrated by Dummar, who contended he found millionaire Howard Hughes wandering in the Nevada desert in 1967 and gave him a ride to Las Vegas. On the basis of this kindness, Hughes was supposed to have wanted to reward Dummar with a fortune, and via mysterious courier, sent Dummar a hand-scrawled will, leaving him a sixteenth of his millions.

Maida spoke to the judge. "Your Honor, this man is a publicity seeker. He's popped up at one notable trial after another. I don't see any point in going further with this."

Grubb's face flamed red, as though he'd never dreamed the man was a phoney. It seemed clear, however, that Forsythe's testimony was supposed to counter Frank Urpman's: He told Grubb he had been making a telephone call from a booth outside the union hall when he saw Silme stumble out the door, "hollerin' his head off for help" and clutching his stomach. Silme, he claimed, did not know who had done it but he knew who was responsible. He described Silme as a "slight" man with an "accent." Terri would later take the stand and shoot down this testimony.

When Maida brought up Forsythe's surprise appearance in the Hughes case, she asked if he would still say he was "the kind of guy who doesn't like to get involved."

"All I came down here to do is tell the facts, and that's what I've done," he answered. After the disclosure about Hughes's will, defense attorneys hadn't much to ask Forsythe, and he was excused.

The next day this article by Timothy Egan appeared in the *Seattle PI*:

"A 'surprise' defense witness in the union murder trial once offered a bizarre plan to help former State Sen. Gordon Walgren in his 'Gamscam' racketeering case, Walgren told the Post Intelligencer yesterday. The witness, Levane Forsythe, approached the former Senate majority leader on a deserted beach last spring with a plan to set him up with electronic gear to help him thwart the FBI, Walgren said. With the new wrinkle in Forsythe's saga yesterday, he now has ties to three recent spectacular trials. 'I'm just in the wrong place at the wrong time, I guess—that's unfortunate for me,' Forsythe said. Defense attorney James Grubb moaned last night that his surprise witness could prove to be the undoing of his case. However, he said he still believed Forsythe's testimony. 'He seems credible to me,' he said. Forsythe lives in the Puget Sound area but left town 'on business' after testifying. He returned home last night and then said he would 'be leaving the state' again today. Asked what he did for a living, Forsythe said, 'I do projects, I put projects together.' Told of Walgren's assertions, Forsythe said, 'Law enforcement scares me to death more than anything.'"

Terri and Cindy read this piece together over coffee the next morning. Terri had stayed over in Ballard, too tired to make it home. In a timely way the piece carried the two women to an obvious conclusion: Forsythe was much more than a publicity seeker. He had to have been a paid witness, and why not for an agency in the State Department?

Mike Withey had the same feeling regarding Forsythe, that his appearance offered a glimpse into the depths of conspiracy the CJDV might be dealing with. Forsythe had showed up late on a Friday, too late to get him on the stand. Years later, when Withey took his desposition for the families' civil trial against Marcos, Forsythe told him that he'd called Joanne Maida on the weekend before he'd testified, asking her to "tell me what she wanted me to say." He admitted that he was taping the conversation, perhaps hoping she'd

144

be caught in an error that would damage the Committee's case. She wasn't taken in by him and when Forsythe came in the following day, Withey knew that he'd appeared in the Hughes trial as the carrier of the fake will that was supposed to enrich Dummar. Forsythe had also appeared in another case, involving Hughes being spirited away from the Desert Inn. He was produced by Robert Mayheu, an ex-FBI and CIA agent, who was supposed to have been part of a plan to assassinate Fidel Castro. Withey was certain they were dealing with someone with powerful connections.

Maida chose to belittle Forsythe's testimony and it was thrown out, but he'd been in a position to obstruct every piece of solid evidence the Committee and the prosecution had against the killers. In his deposition for the civil trial, Forsythe admitted to Withey that he was an agent for both the FBI and the IRS, and that he continued to work for them after the Domingo case. He admitted that he wire-tapped and kept surveillance on people—for instance, out of Alaska. On assignment, he might typically be asked to go to a restaurant and observe—go to a special place and just watch, then tape his observations and send these to a control agent in San Francisco.

Withey deposed Forsythe's control agent for the civil trial and learned that Forsythe, indeed, worked for the FBI and IRS in 1981, and was considered reliable.

Withey came to believe that if Forsythe were sent to witness at the murder trial, then the case—and protecting Baruso—must have mattered greatly to a US agency, and Withey could only imagine this effort was made as a favor to Marcos. But even as early as 1981, Forsythe's appearance seemed to guarantee that the killers were part of a chain leading to Manila.

This was the thesis the Committee for Justice had been developing all along: that people connected to Marcos were behind the assassination of Gene and Silme.

A demonstration was planned to take place in front of the Philippine Consulate before the final defense and prosecution arguments scheduled for the following week. The Committee for Justice felt the timing of the demonstration was right, in order to get their position out prior to the sentencings on which they were counting. They did not think such a demonstration could hurt their case because the jury was sequestered. But the public mind must be touched, and it was crucial to do so now.

WHAT IS THE MARCOS CONNECTION IN THE KILLING

OF SILME AND GENE? read one sign held by Cindy and Lynn. The KDP was out in force as well as a portion of their growing legal team, all prepared for the press, who asked them to explain the connection. Cindy told the reporters, "Marcos benefits by the murders because Silme and Gene were against his regime, his martial law, and because Local 37 had made a definite probe into his hide with their Honolulu resolution ... the US benefits by their deaths because organizing labor in the Philippines would raise export prices and choke off a consistent cheap labor supply." The family also pointed out that while Silme and Gene's opposition of Marcos was often mentioned in regard to the trial, not one word had been printed about how Dictado, Baruso, and the Tulisan supported Marcos.

✻

Benny Guloy surprised everyone by taking the stand as part of the final argument for the defense. He brought an interpreter though his English was fine, his family having been in the US since the sixties. At twenty-two he looked young. He denied everything eloquently, in fact, given the fear that lay over his head like a shadow.

Guloy stated he was Silme's good friend; why would he want to hurt him? Yes, he had stopped by the union hall earlier, to pay Silme back the five dollars he owed him. He'd spent the rest of the day at gambling clubs, right on through the night, except when he stopped by his dad's office, sick with a hangover. At one point he "passed out" from drink. So he hadn't much memory of that period, but just prior he'd been at a club where Jimmy Ramil was dealing. The next day when the police came to his house, they "yelled" at his grandmother, never read him his Miranda rights, pushed him around. Joanne Maida took apart his testimony sentence by sentence.

It was hard to say what effect Guloy's appearance had on the jury. He seemed to make little sense of Silme's having named him as one of the hit men. He said he didn't know why Silme would have done that.

The next day was Ramil's turn. This time, however, Maida asked that the interpreter be dismissed, because Jimmy understood perfectly well what she was saying. Ramil went through the same series of denials as Guloy, insisting, too, that he was a "friend" of Silme. Terri came up later and denied this vehemently.

Ramil "hardly knew Ben Guloy," had never heard of the Tulisan until it was mentioned in the papers, and denied telling San Pablo on May 31 that Dictado was going to have Gene killed the next day. Ramil was one of eighteen witnesses claiming that at the time of the murder, he was dealing hi que at a club in the ID. Some of those witnesses, however, were shown to be related to the suspects, and one woman admitted she owed money to the Tulisan.

Terri watched Ramil step down. Never forget he shot your husband, she reminded herself. It was Ramil's file Gene was holding when he was shot in the back. This ninth-floor courtroom seemed a million miles from Alaska, yet how real and connected it was to so many lives up there.

With the official end of summer, Joanne Maida began her systematic attack on Guloy and Ramil's credibility. If the jury believed her, the defendants were the lowest of the low: You'd never find any homicide as base as killing for hire, never a gun so ugly, never a cause so maligned. These men may have known Silme, may have liked him. But they killed him precisely in the line of business. And Gene and Silme were murdered because they believed in union reform. They were good men. She reminded the jury that Silme was the first Filipino Phi Beta Kappa to graduate from the University of Washington. "It is on his strength, his honesty, and his integrity that this case is built.

"When Silme named his killers, he named them with all the strength and wit left him, drained as he was of blood, fighting waves of shock. Naming his killers was a courageous act." Listening to the prosecutor, Terri imagined once more her husband on the street, wrapping what was left of himself to his middle, one thought in mind: Get the killers and end this terror.

"If his final words meant anything at all," Maida concluded, "Guloy and Ramil must be convicted of murder." She left it quite clear that, although they were not acting alone, they murdered Silme and Gene.

The families couldn't wait for Grubb's argument and tentatively planned a party appropriate to the release they knew they'd feel when the verdict came in. They had to win this one; it was so basic. So much of what they stood for was hanging by a thread—not only their politics, but the reform plan, which existed at the gut level prior to politics. These values had to be validated by a favorable verdict.

Grubb went after Silme's condition once again, saying that naming the men after being hit four times by "the ugliest weapon I've ever seen" was "John Wayne stuff." Then he returned to Forsythe, telling the jury he was convinced Forsythe had told the truth, that he was where he claimed to have been, and heard Silme say he "did not know" who his killers were. Regarding Forsythe's part in the Mormon will, Grubb said, "I must admit, I was as shocked to learn about it as you were."

❋

The next day, as the judge read the guilty verdict, Ade Domingo exploded into tears. Embracing Cindy and Terri, she looked about the courtroom to locate Ben Guloy's mother. Ade ran into Mrs. Guloy in the lobby where she'd just arrived, never having been informed that the verdict was coming in that soon. Mrs. Guloy sobbed, "My son is not guilty, my son is not guilty. Lies! So many lies!" Ade moved close to her and touched her arm.

"Now we have both lost sons," she said.

Ade Domingo's remark summed up her feelings more than anything else she might have said. Those hostile to her in the Filipino community insisted her words to Guloy's mother were tinged with anger, revenge her prime motivation. This accusation would grow more pointed during proceedings against Tony Dictado, and years later, regarding Marcos's gang and estate, people would ask Ade, "why don't you stop? Silme is never going to live again, even if you have your victory. Or do you just want an eye for an eye, a tooth for a tooth?" Ade would answer, "It still hurts. And it's justice for Silme I'm seeking, not an eye for an eye. How would you feel if it was your son? Maybe in time I can forgive because I am a Christian, a believer in God, but no way can I forget."

The experience of never forgetting aged Ade, turned a believing woman into a cynic. "Silme has fulfilled God's will," her own mother told her. "Now you must give up this crusade and accept what God knows is right." From family as far away as Cebu to friends Ade counted on in Seattle came advice aimed at curing what they saw as a sickness—but what she knew was her central strength. Friends who rallied in the past now found it difficult to come to the Domingo house for a cup of coffee, even when Ade implored them to keep her company. Having decided her course was right, she became a pariah, and the more Cindy studied cases like theirs, the more she understood that her mother—and the rest of the family—would be negatively labeled by an unadoring public.

Shortly after the verdict, a *Seattle Times* article by Dick Clever quoted Guloy's father: "I know my boy, no way he could have done it. He couldn't even slaughter a chicken. And those fellows were Communists, you know."

Some thought even the prosecutor, who'd done a fine job of taking the case down its gang-versus-union alley, had little political sympathy for the families. And the most nagging question concerning the state still remained: Why had the US Attorney suggested immunity for Baruso? That tactic would never rest with any member of the Domingo family or the legal team.

The night after the verdict, gathered at their house with friends dropping by and the legal team mapping a strategy for the next stage, Ade found a quiet moment with Cindy at the side of the crowd. "Do you know what that snake tried with me last September?" Her daughter had no idea what she was talking about. "Baruso, when your dad and me was having tough times. He picks me up, tells me he wants to take care of me. Dad's good friend. Drives me around, says I can talk to him and all this stuff. Stops at a motel!" She whispered with emphasis, then looked around at the guests drinking and talking in clusters. "Wants to know if I want to go in 'to talk.' I say, 'hell no, and take me home.' I was so mad I couldn't even be scared."

Cindy looked into her mother's eyes. "There are lots of reasons for wanting to get him up on the stand again."

Especially after Ade's revelation that night, Cindy often wondered, along with so many others, whose imprisonment— Baruso's or Dictado's—would give them the most satisfaction for Silme and Gene's murders? It became an increasingly difficult question during those despairing years of the early 1980s, when President Reagan was constantly violating the rights of minorities and broadening the base of conservative wealth. Must Reagan be ousted before indicting Marcos?

Baruso bragged of connections all the way to Marcos; the Committee for Justice knew their job was to unravel those ties. Who had Baruso talked with in Hawaii just prior to returning home in May? For many people, imagining the take-down of Marcos was like trying to hit a tarantula long-range with a BB gun.

Nevertheless, there was something oddly soft about the other side, as though the defense was actually bent on self-destruction. For instance, Dictado's lawyer. It took all spring of 1982 to get Dictado to face trial. On the way, he fired one lawyer and hired James Grubb, who represented Ramil. A bad choice, everyone agreed.

The prosecutor pointed out that hiring Grubb was counterproductive because during Ramil's trial, Grubb had repeatedly hinted that Dictado was the real culprit. Guloy's attorney had made that claim outright. And if, as seemed already clear, Grubb planned to free Dictado by insisting Ramil was the actual gunman, how could he then work for Ramil, who had yet to be sentenced? The judge ruled with the prosecutor, and Grubb was dismissed from the case. The act bought time, but it also further tarnished Dictado's case.

Dictado hired a young lawyer named John Henry Browne. The trial was supposed to last for weeks, but testimony took only a few days. Again, Robert San Pablo was the unflinching witness, this time insisting that Tony Dictado told him three or four times that he planned to kill Gene Viernes. Dictado had asked San Pablo about Gene's car and his work hours. And again San Pablo implicated Ramil, repeating that Ramil had approached him outside a restaurant and told him Dictado was going to kill Gene. He added two more bombshells: Dictado had offered to pay Guloy and Ramil $5,000 apiece for the killing, and Boy Pilay had told him that Baruso planned to pay Dictado $5,000 for his part in the crime.

Dictado, in an attempt to reach the hearts of the jury, broke into sobs when his lawyer asked if he were afraid for his children in the Philippines. Tony said he "knew plenty" but couldn't say a word for fear they'd be killed. His words, his tears, his certainty that his children's lives would be threatened simply deepened the case against him. If he were hiding information vital to the case, he was an accessory after facts that might implicate Baruso's connections inside the US government. And Dictado admitted to lying during the previous trial by locating Ramil and Guloy at the Old Timer's Club at the time of the murders, eradicating any doubt the sentencing judge might have had about them.

Dictado admitted he had spoken to Baruso two days before the murders. It wasn't the forty-minute-long talk claimed by the state, but there was a "discussion." He appeared to be gripped by a cord leading through a maze of corruption to Baruso and the Philippine consulate in Hawaii, from there perhaps to someone in charge of hit men, someone like General Fabian Ver, the most vigorous of Marcos's avengers.

In order to get near their obvious enemies, the families and their lawyers knew they had to find friends on the other side. The legal team connected with one US agent they thought might be willing to provide phone records proving that Baruso had called the US consulate shortly after the murders. Terri was sure Baruso must have talked to someone when he left meetings abruptly, only to return with more ammunition against the union reformists.

Meanwhile, Dictado was sentenced to Walla Walla, out of sight and mind, though the papers did a brilliant job of making him look—as his attorney insisted—the victim of his boss, Tony Baruso, and Robert San Pablo. Despite the weeping court, the four-column picture of heartbroken women at Dictado's back and his ten-month-old son now fatherless, the Domingos knew they had stormed beyond the Tulisan: One more furious lawyer was shouting that Baruso had planned it all.

Yet they could not smile or laugh with the gaiety they had known only a year before. Send Dictado up, Cindy thought, send him all the way up. She and Terri got drunk one mid-May weekend, after that swaggering bully was found guilty of murder. People gathered in Ade's garden, the sun shining on her blooming azaleas and rhododendrons. Soon no one could distinguish one child's howling or laughter from another's. Terri fell asleep on a blanket in the sun and woke to hear Shari Woo saying, "I dreamed I saw Silme last night." Fuzzy with wine, Cindy and Terri squinted at their friend. "It was clear as day. I was in Kane Hall. He walked down that Gothic hallway, took a seat beside me for the lecture, and said, 'Don't be sad, Shari, I'm alive, we fooled those suckers.'"

The three women sat in the drooping sun, wiping tears. Terri finally said, "I dream about him, too."

"Me too," Cindy nodded, reminiscing. "Once in college he asked me to retake a Classics exam for him, to better his grade. 'The professor'll never know the difference; all Filipinos look alike,'" she quoted Silme's mocking voice. Later, after Silme got a B, she told him he should let her wear his Phi Beta Kappa key.

❋

The following Monday, the Domingos were right back at it, anxious to start their next proceeding: the first memorial of Gene and Silme's deaths. The memorial would tie in with Cultural Night of the Far West Convention, which five hundred people were expected to attend.

Terri felt much better now that three gang members were behind bars. The reformed union had recalled Tony Baruso from office long ago, after showing that he'd been moving their funds around to his

151

own benefit. Soon they would mount a civil suit charging him with embezzlement, but they were still short of the murder charge.

Terri, Cindy, and the Committee for Justice hoped the power of the throngs attending the memorial would bring down an army of doubt. During the course of the evening a moving videotape was shown, including views of Local 37's hiring hall (soon to be extinct) and scenes of men and women in Alaskan canneries, hunkered over tables sliming fish. Then an enlarged photo of Silme and Gene appeared, the two smiling friends flanking an aging Filipino worker like bookends. Terri didn't care who saw her weep.

Tears were consoling, but they did not salve the loneliness. She tried writing down some of her thoughts in a half-empty notebook she'd found, started while she was still in high school. Her daughter, Ligaya, wanted to know what she was writing about. Standing in the doorway, she asked Terri if she wrote about Daddy.

"No," Terri said, "I'm just jotting down notes for a press conference."

Ligaya's face clouded over. "Does that mean we'll be in the papers again?"

Terri frowned. "Is the publicity getting to be too much for you?"

"I'm tougher, Mom." As Ligaya moved past her mother into the kitchen, she touched her leg.

"Is it hard in school? Kids give you a rough time?"

"No. I told my teacher Marcos did it, that one day we're gonna get him."

"What did she say?"

"Said it's not been proved yet."

Somehow, hearing Ligaya quote her teacher made Terri relax. "Guess she's right, huh? At least for now."

"Maybe." The girl turned. "That's your old diary. Are you lonely, Mom?"

Terri nodded.

"Will you ever ... go out?"

"I haven't thought about it." Why not tell her the truth? The papers called her Silme's "live-in girlfriend," "mother to his daughters." They'd never print it that way again, after she called them and said she was Silme's "wife, goddamnit!"

"It's your life," Ligaya said, and ran down the stairs and outside to play with her sister.

❁

152

Holding press conferences was a tactical maneuver to keep the case developing. On August 6, the Committee was anxious to speak to the media. They held up a huge picture of Terri carrying her youngest, Kalayaan, thumb in mouth, and another of Cindy looking angry. They asked their central question: How is it that Baruso had never been charged with murder? And, in connection, what had the FBI done to help the union stop high-stakes gambling in the canneries? Lawyers for the victims' families filed a civil suit for murder on the eve of the Marcoses' planned visit with the Reagans in the White House. The suit charged Tony Baruso as a US agent working closely with the Philippine government, which also was charged. The legal team now had documented evidence of visits made by Baruso to the Filipino consulate after the conference in April 1981. He also had visited the Philippines recently and was admitted to Marcos on a first-name basis. Through an unnamed agent, the team gained evidence that Baruso placed three calls to the State Department shortly after the murders. And they had San Pablo's testimony that Boy Pilay had told him Baruso was paying others to have Silme and Gene killed. Baruso had obtained a high-level security clearance from the US in order to access classified information on anti-Marcos opposition.

In presenting the civil suit, Mike Withey had wanted to charge Ferdinand Marcos. The judge at first dismissed Marcos as head of a foreign power, but allowed the Philippine government to remain in the suit. This break was a key, because it granted the legal team subpoena power against Philippine agents, and subsequently Withey was able to examine Tony Baruso's travel records, bank statements, and charge card transactions. He discovered that on May 17, 1981, only two weeks before the murders and shortly after the Hawaii convention, Baruso had traveled to San Francisco and stayed at the Sutter Hotel near the Philippine consulate. Shortly after this move, a mysterious $10,000 deposit appeared on his bank statement. For the Committee this clue tied Baruso to San Francisco, possibly to the Mabuhay Corporation, which operated pro-Marcos radio stations in the Bay Area, and during the time of Baruso's visit, had piped an ad by Marcos via TV satellite into a spacious hall, after which assembled guests could exchange pleasantries with his image on the screen.

Details of the case began to resemble a murder mystery. In August a Seattle newspaper suggested that filing the suit on the eve of Marcos's visit looked like "a ploy for publicity," and that the Committee's theory of conspiracy sounded like "fiction."

153

Terri called Cindy to learn if she'd seen this editorial; Cindy had already copied the piece for their archives. "Of course it's a ploy for publicity!" Terri shouted. And they were the ones creating a *fiction*? Not the Marcos regime? Not Imelda Marcos for shopping like an orgiast? Not Reagan for praising Marcos's record on human rights, or Marcos for calling Reagan "God's anointed?"

That same week, Rene Cruz arrived in Seattle with Isabel Letelier, who was in mourning for her husband Orlando, who had been assassinated in Washington, DC, in 1976. His murderers were Chilean thugs, undetained by the INS when they entered the US. The Letelier assassination made perfectly plain the price of speaking out against Pinochet—or Marcos—in the US. Marcos and his wife requested that Reagan extradite Rene Cruz, and others who shared his views, for publicly airing distrust of the Philippine government. Though Cruz, a Filipino national, had lived in the US for years, no one knew how Reagan might respond to his friends' request.

At times like these, clear thinking was an exhausting practice. It was difficult enough for Terri to raise the girls alone, to keep going to work, to file this suit against Marcos. But the thinking required to reduce Marcos's injustices, to translate his madness into legal language, often left her brain muddled. At the end of each day, she toppled into bed, sleep swallowing her within minutes. Then, awake at four every morning, fear enveloping her, she'd get out of bed and stare at her own exhausted face in the mirror. With tremulous fingers, she'd trace the fine lines etched into her forehead, spreading out from the corners of her eyes. Might the evil she had seen, daily was coached to understand, have gotten inside and turned her into a likeness of her enemies? During the months since Silme's death, she constantly whirled with necessary tasks, but when given a moment of reflection, her mind easily opened upon alleys of despair.

Terri believed nothing worked for the truly lonely but to get through each day. Every morning she must get to First Avenue and Cedar, then to the mountains seen from her office window. Those mountains were a real place, neither lonely nor despairing, snow capping granite. One day she would get to them, bringing her girls with her.

❄

While their suit was still pending, Terri called Cindy with news that Mike Withey had heard that Boy Pilay was back in town. To have Pilay back within their grasp was a moving prospect. He had testified at the first trial, but afterwards had been released from custody for "lack of evidence." When subpoenaed to appear at the Dictado trial, he had run, apparently to his family in Maryland. While visiting Washington, DC, to attend a meeting, Withey picked up a Baltimore phone book and checked for Domingues. There were three, so he dialed and on the first try, asking, "Is Boy home?" got Boy's mother, who told him, no, he was out for the night. Withey called Joanne Maida immediately and asked for his arrest, giving her the address from the phone book. It took two weeks for this arrest to take place. A SWAT team surrounded the house, but they reported that, although someone left the house and drove off in a car, they hadn't pursued because "he didn't limp."

Back in Seattle, Withey learned that Boy was hanging around the 609 Club in the International District. Withey took up a room in the Bush Hotel, trying to learn of Boy's movements with binoculars. Spotting him one night, Withey again called Maida, asking her, please, not to send in the FBI. Lynn Domingo called Withey shortly afterward to say she'd learned that two tall white men, wearing suits and thin ties, had walked into 609, asked for Boy Pilay, and were told he'd left. Withey was devastated, but as soon as he'd hung up the phone, he spotted Pilay once more. Pilay apparently had not seen the two agents. He was arrested shortly afterwards.

Cindy didn't know why Boy Pilay had returned to Seattle, though there was much speculation. Maybe, while back East, he'd been touched by members of the gang, or had some score to settle, or wanted finally to get paid for his part in the murders. How much Baruso actually had paid anyone was open to question; Cindy suspected Guloy and Ramil had been stiffed because Silme had named them. Dictado must have gotten $5,000, but what about Boy Pilay? Would he risk coming home on this account? Perhaps he dreamed of being Baruso's man on the level now left vacant by Dictado.

He was in and they had him; the bail was good-sized. Both Cindy and Terri pleaded with their lawyers, trying to understand. How had Pilay been released after the first trial when he'd been described as the courier carrying a death threat to Alaska? Why had the police arrested him if nothing might come of his appearance here? If he had a key role in revealing Tony Baruso was behind the murders,

155

and Baruso was being protected, then what use was he to the prosecutor, who seemed to be doing everything right except arresting Baruso?

Five days after his arrest, Pilay was free, again for lack of evidence, though the deputy prosecutor still insisted the investigation was "continuing." The families protested and Withey called it a "serious travesty of justice," but Pilay remained free. Via rumor, they followed him to White Center, to gambling clubs, to all his old haunts. Like Benny Guloy, he was only a kid, and seemed to have no idea what fury he was dealing with—unless he'd been forced to come back by those who thought they were above the law. But what innocence, if he'd come willingly, so blind to the havoc the Tulisan had in store for him.

In late November 1982, Withey warned the prosecutor, "he'll be dead before the year's out, and you'll be partly responsible." Withey was a little off; Boy Pilay was murdered in the middle of January 1983, less than two months later.

When Terri looked back to that time, flipped through her diary to the days just prior to Boy Pilay's violent passing, she saw two revealing entries written on the day before he was murdered. The first was a note regarding documents given in support of their civil suit, the proof of Baruso's three conversations with the State Department within twenty-four hours of Gene and Silme's murders. Terri had specified the lengths of the calls and indicated there were two reliable insiders whose names the legal team couldn't divulge; her notes reminded the court of Baruso's bragging that he knew Marcos personally and was, effectively, an operative working to harass those who fought Marcos in the US.

The second entry concerned a call from Cindy. She had wanted to know if Terri had seen Rick Anderson's column in the *Times* that Sunday. Anderson had written about Tony Dictado in the Walla Walla State Penitentiary, calling out to Jesus and evoking his "minister" with every other choking phrase. From his cell he cried injustice: "'I was tired reading every article where those Communists are saying things about me. And it's about time the public hears my side of the story. Not only those Communists who lied in my trial.'"

Dictado asserted he wasn't read his rights, that he'd been harassed to plead second-degree if he'd talk, but he couldn't plea bargain because he never did murder anybody. And, remember, his kids had been threatened. Anderson didn't know if Dictado would ever "find his voice," but wrote that he had found the "agony of prison life

156

without a future," concluding, "Dictado's words may mean something to anyone who doubts the despair of prison; they also may bring vengeful cheer to the relatives of Viernes and Domingo, for if the state will not kill him ... maybe he might do the thing himself."

Terri's diary note read: Is this man serious?

Terri's note also mentioned that Dictado had written to Cindy. "Hi Cindy. How are you? I am okay. Things are kinda lonely here." She did not write back, nor did she tell her mother—Ade would have had a fit.

But the real point of Terri remembering was the timing of her announcement of the Civil Suit, which made the papers on January 16, 1983, and coincided with Anderson's column.

Boy Pilay had been shot through the head several times, his body dumped in a blackberry patch near a grade school in South Park the day after her diary entries. One man arrested for the murder had a built-in "revenge" motive; the other had run for the Philippines. Both had worked at University Hospital.

Pilay's death occurred a month after the US government had shoved aside the case against Marcos for the time being, granting him immunity from prosecution in the civil suit for murder. The US had denied the Letelier precedent, a law stating that foreign powers are not immune from lawsuits in cases where "money is sought for personal injury or death occurring in the United States." The families certainly were seeking money: $30 million, a portion of which, if awarded, would be used to set up a fund to further the work that Silme and Gene had started.

A fatal knowledge was spreading among the members of the Committee for Justice, the sort of knowledge, which, if absorbed, could destroy their belief in several trusted institutions and individuals at once. But this sort of knowing loomed even larger, threatening to separate them from the average man or woman, an alienating power that could make their friends shun, even despise them.

Terri visited the Ballard Locks one blustery winter afternoon. As she watched the big ships move alongside the small ones, she saw Silme moving toward her in the rain. She lifted her face to greet him, but it wasn't him. It was a boy, years younger than she could ever remember being, who looked at her oddly as he walked past. Standing there alone with only the ships for company, Terri thought, "I'm too young to know what I know. If only I could be ignorant again, for just a day, then maybe I could rest." Slowly and carefully, she drove back across town to her children.

Wapato
Summer 1983

Cindy sensed what Gene must have felt the many times he traveled this route over Manashtash Pass and down the long backbone forming the Yakima Valley. As she passed Union Gap, a fairyland of fruit trees opened below her. It had been hard enough remembering Silme these past months; just last week, after the long haul of dragging their civil suit by the yokes on their necks, she had been hit with the realization that Gene, too, was her brother. She knew she would see him again in many of Wapato's faces.

Andy had called her. "Let's get all the family down here some weekend for a pig roast—maybe a rodeo!" Now, the valley burst with life, and Andy's suggestion seemed a way to lighten the heaviness of meeting only at funerals, memorials and trials. Driving past trailer parks, down the sandy streets behind Wapato High, Cindy looked for the spot at the edge of the orchards where so many Vierneses and Pascuas lived. She saw Andy standing in front of his house, waving, then Gene's sister Barbara, and his mom Betty, whose hair had turned very gray.

Andy wrapped his arms around Cindy and lifted her off the ground. Behind them, Barbara smiled. Gene's death had cost his sister one job; she hadn't been able to think clearly for months. It was good to see her looking more relaxed. Betty's face resembled a desert landscape, wisdom in every line. She invited Cindy into her house. "This is Scrabble day," Betty said. "You want to play?"

The Scrabble board lay on the kitchen table. With so many faces and so much interacting, Cindy felt as though she'd entered a friendly village rather than a house. As they sat down to coffee, Andy flipped on the TV to watch a wrestling match with his kids, and Gene's older sister, Patty, pushed into the kitchen and enthused over the Scrabble board.

Butting out her cigarette, Patty stared at Cindy, while Cindy remembered roaring through Death Valley with Gene the summer he stayed in Oakland, and afterwards driving to Las Vegas to see Patty. That was when Patty had inadvertently flipped a scoop of ice cream over her daughter's head, and Gene had grabbed it midair and taken a huge bite. They had all laughed hysterically. Now Patty was frowning, trying to place Cindy. Barbara said, "Silme's sister," and immediately Patty's eyes welled up and she left the room.

Searching for a vowel, Betty assured her guest that Patty would be all right, that whenever she was reminded of Gene she lost control. When Patty came back, she briefly touched Cindy's shoulder before reaching eagerly for her seven tiles.

Later, that day struck Cindy as something out of Alice in Wonderland, especially the looks of doubt she saw on their faces when she brought up the civil suit against Marcos. Barbara understood; she had been named as a co-plaintiff. Everyone understood the process, Cindy thought, but the skepticism of these decent people caused her to doubt, also, and reminded her that she was not at home. Mentioning help from Seattle's progressive mayor, Charles Royer, might be an instant hit in Ballard, but not here. This was not the kitchen of the Domingos, who ate politics with their breakfast. It was as if the people in this tough little farm town were saying, "Hold on, let's take our leisure a step at a time. Surely you Domingos are good enough union folk to know that Saturday means no work shall be done." Quickly Cindy stopped talking about her work, and went for a double-letter blue square.

Later, when Nemesio Jr. arrived, Andy coaxed him into a truck already loaded with Cindy, Gene's brother Steve, another young woman, and a number of young men crammed into the truck bed. A half-barrel beside him on the seat, another friend drove a VW beetle which the truck followed into the sagebrush to a large corral surrounded by skinny bleachers filled with people. Horses munched sparse grass nearby, and a pen full of steer calves cried pitifully out of tune with a tied-up, squealing pig.

A child tugged a donkey over to the crowd, and one of Gene's female relatives told Cindy that traditionally the rodeo couldn't start until a guest rode the donkey around the track. Another member of the family assured Cindy of the donkey's sweet disposition. Cindy looked pleadingly toward Nemesio, but he'd already goaded his two children into cheering for their aunt.

There was no saddle; luckily Cindy was wearing jeans. The donkey was gentle as a lamb, Andy assured her, then lifted her on and aimed the beast in the direction of two big mares trotting in half-circles and snorting. One of the riders whacked her horse's side with a quoit.

The donkey wouldn't budge. Cindy gripped its bristly mane. "Andy, don't hit it!" she yelled, but he switched the donkey's legs and it took off with Cindy bent backwards, her legs sticking straight out on either side of its rib cage. The crowd hollered with glee. The donkey's legs struck the dirt like stilts against concrete; Cindy slid first to the left, then leaned in. All of a sudden, the donkey bucked. The cheers crescendoed as Cindy flew through the air and came down hard in the dust. By the time Andy got to her, she had spit the grit from her mouth and wiped her face with the red bandana she'd bought that morning in Ellensburg.

Cindy stood for a while with a beer, watching the donkey munch hay, reminded of Gene's letter from the Philippines about a donkey's spiked hair against his legs. From a distance she watched Gene's brother working a calf with a rope. He jumped from the pony, hit the ground, and slid with the calf in the dust. She pictured Gene as he might have been if he'd never left this place, never gotten educated in politics. She shook the thought from her head. That kind of thinking was an indictment of their own lives, and made the Domingos responsible for Gene's death. Still, at the first memorial, she'd heard Betty say, "If Felix had never brought him up to Alaska, he'd be here now." Betty's was one kind of truth, one she must live with until she accepted the fact that Gene had been a natural leader.

The brutal heat of the day passed into evening coolness. Several friends gathered close to the Yakima River, and Cindy listened to its rhythm beat against the call of birds flitting among the surrounding fruit trees. People drank wine before a roaring fire of trash wood that smelled of mesquite. Meat cooked over a glowing barbeque pit, while a red sun passed behind Mt. Adams.

❊

Andy brought Cindy a cup of sweet wine, the big man asking how she wanted her meat cooked. All the young Filipinos from Wapato were big and athletic and lived in this landscape as though it had always been theirs. Their families had been in the valley since 1918, three generations at least. Filipinos had organized against race riots ten years after arriving. Wapato took each of its children seriously, as though each one was part of a larger family. A lean boy, Gene's nephew, approached Cindy shyly with a plate of meat. He had the same black eyes, the same fair skin. A couple of kids were riding bikes, doing wheelies around the fire, the light glancing off chrome spokes and white teeth.

If Wapato saw Gene differently than Seattle, that was only natural. "We used to do stuff that was just insane," Andy remembered. "The cops raided us when we were in college,

160

everybody going out the window, the wrestling team kind of booking together. This one guy looks back at the cops and runs right into a tree.

"It knocks him out, the bark cuts him all up. We pick him up and keep running. When he comes to and touches his bloody face, he says, 'Goddamn, what happened to me?' Gene says, 'The damn cops were beating the shit out of you. We managed to save your ass.'

"But this guy's a real hothead—he goes back and fights the cop! They arrest him, we have to go down and bail him out. 'God,' I said to Gene, 'how could you do that?'

"'I didn't know the guy was going to go back.'"

In his quiet voice, Andy told another anecdote of their friendship. "One time in Alaska Gene and I stole all this salmon. I don't know what we were thinking. We went back to the warehouse and took it after the others had left. Then we thought, what do we do with fifteen cases of fish? Finally we threw it out the window, thinking we were safe. Next morning, like a hundred yards away, there're these shiny cans of salmon laying all over the beach."

❄

Six days after returning from Wapato, on August 21, 1983, Cindy stood, dumbfounded, watching international TV with Terri, as Ninoy Aquino was escorted by Philippine agents onto the tarmac of Manila Airport and gunned down before the eyes of the world.

The Domingo family spent the next few days watching television, reading Time Magazine, Seattle and Hawaiian dailies, and running up phone bills to the KDP in Oakland and Berkeley, in an attempt to keep abreast of events after Ninoy's assassination. Everyone, from left-wing activists to Reagan's spokespeople agreed the killing had to be the work of either Ferdinand Marcos and General Ver or Imelda and her demented brother Kokoy. If Marcos and his wife were split on the matter—a possibility based in part on a rumor that he had hit her in the jaw when he heard the news—the bloody blunder could only work in the families' favor. With Ninoy's death the enormous opposition to Marcos was no longer willing to keep quiet, and the families watched the political scene in the Philippines with an eye toward improving their position. How strange that his assassination, followed by the toppling of the oligarchy, was precisely the event which aided them in their effort to prove their suit against Marcos.

161

The Civil Suit:
The Families of Domingo & Viernes vs. the Marcos Estate
Seattle
1989

At the heart of the Domingo/Viernes civil suit was a solid legal team, a complex of singular attitudes held by a number of remarkable people. Mike Withey, the primary attorney, worked with especial zeal for having directly experienced the wholesale injustice of the Marcos regime: the murder of two good friends. Joining him were Jeffery Robinson, a black attorney aware of the casual terror of the Reagan administration, and Liz Schott and Jim Douglas, both from Evergreen Legal Services.

The key event working in favor of the Committee for Justice and the legal team occurred in 1986 when Marcos was knocked from power and sought refuge at Hickman Air Force Base in Honolulu. Withey flew to Hawaii to take Marcos's deposition and was given access to Marcos's records, which had been seized by US customs when he landed on US soil. Among these documents were papers relating to the Mabuhay Corporation. One included several lines in Dr. Leonilo Malabed's hand stating that he had received $1 million under authority of General Fabian Ver for intelligence operations in the US. The statement detailed what monies had been spent, and for what purposes—such as contributions to both Ronald Reagan's and Jimmy Carter's campaigns. And there, on May 17, 1981, the same day that Baruso's records showed him flying to San Francisco, was an outlay of $15,000 for an item called "special security." With that discovery, Withey and the Committee for Justice were convinced they had vital evidence enabling them to win the case, and to reveal the truth about the Marcos's government's repressive abuse of the Filipino people.

An important legal advisor to the families was John Caughlan, an activist lawyer who had fought against Filipino deportations in the fifties. He thought that some of the more interesting implications of the case related to the political climate in the Philippines after Marcos's expulsion to Hawaii and subsequent death from kidney failure in September 1989. During the trial Caughlan was host to Bonifacio Gillego, newly elected to the Philippine congress and one of the families' witnesses. Gillego was pessimistic about the Philippines' future. He realized that Ninoy Aquino's widow,

Corazon, enjoyed immense popular support. But he also felt the forces surrounding her were incapable of making the reforms necessary to allow the Philippines to become a genuinely independent, democratic nation, much like Latin American nations in which the ruling elite controlled masses of people in desperate poverty.

Boni Gillego, who earlier had disproved the myth that Marcos had been generously decorated during World War II, encouraged the pursuit of the families' case even though he knew a court might find it difficult to rule against the Philippines now that Marcos was dead. Richard Hibey, Marcos's lawyer, pleaded with the jury not to judge in favor of the plaintiffs solely on the basis of their feelings against his clients. But he never pointed out the possible unfairness of ruling in the millions of dollars against a country with no money in its treasury. Anticipating this, the Committee for Justice declared that, regardless of the sum, any money possibly won would be used to help right the losses suffered by the victim's families.

The most important part of the legal team's role in serving this case properly was to get hundreds of people thinking along the same lines. They had to be made to believe that a conspiracy ran from Local 37's president to the Philippine Consulate to the State Department, and that money for the assassinations came from Manila via San Francisco and Hawaii. This task was made easier every time a CIA operation was laid bare by convincing witnesses such as Ralph McGehee, a former CIA operative, who stated on the stand that paranoid governments really do perform ugly deeds in the name of national security.

The next crucial step was to convince the jury that Gene Viernes and Silme Domingo worked at jobs important enough to get them killed, despite Richard Hibey's assertion that Silme and Gene, "though admirable men, doing admirable work," nevertheless "labored in a smaller vineyard." It was just this line of thought—that Silme and Gene were small-fry, union joes—that had turned people against this case for eight years. How could anyone such as Marcos, with his money, influence, and grandeur, fear these two enough to have them murdered?

The Trial
Seattle
Fall 1989

Judge Barbara Rothstein pushed her glasses higher on the bridge of her nose. She appeared bored with the plaintiff's line of questioning. "Mr. Savage," she addressed Tony Baruso's lawyer, "would you advise your client that he may answer counsel's question?"

Baruso, his dark hair showing gray, wore a handsome tweed coat and striped tie. His questioner, young Jeff Robinson, appeared relaxed and ready to resume. "Now, Mr. Baruso, let's do this theoretically."

Savage wanted the judge to clarify Robinson's question.

"He's going to ask something hypothetically."

"May we try, Your Honor?" Robinson asked. "The example will be painlessly easy."

The judge nodded. Baruso leaned forward, stony-faced.

"Now, Mr. Baruso, if Ade Domingo—Silme Domingo's mother— for example, were to say you had bragged on many occasions that you were a close friend of Ferdinand Marcos, that you had a picture of him shaking hands with you in your office—"

"What's the relevance, Your Honor?"

"Proceed."

"—and that you were very interested in the activities of the KDP, would you then say that Ade Domingo was a liar?"

"Yes!" Baruso exploded. "She's a liar! Ade Domingo's a liar!"

Baruso's lawyer cringed as the venomous reply reached the jury box.

"And if Dave Della or Robert Santos were to say that you had claimed to be a good friend of Marcos, would you say that they were lying?"

"Yes! Them, too, both of them, damned liars!" Tony's high-pitched bleat brought derisive laughter from the crowd lining the walls.

The judge sat back in her chair, adjusting her glasses. "Mr. Robinson, do you have any further theoretical questions for the witness?"

"Thanks, Your Honor," Robinson said, "that'll be all for now."

Baruso left the box and walked imperiously toward a seat beside his lawyer. Cindy Domingo, her eyes blinking behind recently acquired contact lenses, exchanged a glance with her mother seated next to her. Ade shook her head and whispered, "I thought I'd heard everything."

The jury was comprised of three men and three women who had been instructed that this was not a criminal trial but a civil suit in which one had to prove monetary damages as a result of a conspiracy to murder. The complaint read: "The murders were but one overt act of a broader tortious conspiracy to surveil, harass and intimidate the class of anti-Marcos Filipinos in the United States." The jury was being asked to determine if Baruso had arranged the murders on behalf of the Philippine government.

One slightly overweight, bearded juror in his forties, wearing a checked flannel shirt, had nodded so vigorously while Robinson interrogated Baruso that his entire body looked to be in agreement with the attorney's methods and results. Next to him, the face of a middle-aged, expensively coifed woman drooped to the collar of her red dress. Another woman sat next to her, also in her fifties with white-gray hair, but she looked relaxed and attentive, taking notes. The three other jurors included a businesswoman and two men in their twenties, one named Bible from Port Angeles, the other a drama student at Western Washington State University.

Steve Psinakis, who had married into a prominent family in the Philippines, testified early in the trial. Along with his wife, Prisilla Lopez, they had run an opposition newspaper until they came under the wrath of Marcos. Psinakis was forced to leave his family in the Philippines and to relocate in San Francisco. Psinakis supported anti-Marcos organizations in the US. In 1980, within Imelda Marcos's Waldorf Astoria suite, he had been bribed and threatened when he refused to drop his campaign against Marcos.

Not long before the trial, on an early, wet Sunday morning in San Francisco, Psinakis noticed a car tailing him. The vehicle pulled up to the curb next to his, and the passenger gestured to him to roll down his window. Suddenly the man was holding a pistol against his temple. Psinakis clamped his foot down on the accelerator and fled.

Raul Manglapus' political career stretched back to the years of Magsaysay's rule. He was against the presence of US bases in the Philippines. His testimony, which had been taped, was piped into the courtroom by video. The result was not as effective as Psinakis's live testimony; nevertheless, he described regular photographing and monitoring of anyone engaged in activity that the Marcos regime considered detrimental to its cause.

Bart Alconcel, of the Filipino Consulate in Hawaii, testified by deposition that it was true that the consulate had a list of labor leaders and University of Hawaii professors considered threats to Marcos's rule under martial law. Their phones were bugged and they were monitored at every protest march or demonstration, the information shipped weekly to the Philippines to be groomed by Marcos agents. Did Marcos take a personal interest in this material? As one of the families' lawyers put it, a leader so obsessed with the detail of oligarchy—Marcos selected even the color of the municipal buses—must certainly have taken an active interest in the names and characters of those working against him, at home and abroad.

Through two godsons involved in the labor movement, Marcos used to arrange to have crowds of sympathetic followers on hand whenever he flew into Honolulu. These extras were paid, minimally, of course, but Marcos had stars such as Reagan on his side, and no need to pay him. Reagan believed in Marcos so thoroughly, he took from the US treasury yearly to keep the dictator and his wife secure.

But the one ruling Marcos desired most from Reagan—the extradition of unruly Filipinos living in the US—he was never able to swing. Still, agents of both countries exchanged data, and lies. One of these lies, that Gene Viernes was "carrying $290,000" when he came to the Philippines in March 1981, was potent enough to cause the murders of two young men. When Marcos arrested KMU leaders Felix Olalia and Crispin Beltran in 1982, the charges against them concerned the importation of large sums of money to fight Marcos's rule. But the amount of cash Viernes carried when he traveled to Manila was closer to $2,900.

Marcos's estate put together a very weak case. Perhaps believing in a dictator all those years had given his supporters a sense of invulnerability. By video, Marcos testified that "no one was ever put in jail in my country because of his political opinion." And again, the proclamation of martial law was based on "provisions of the constitution." Even his enemies approved. Benigno Aquino had told him, "Of course you should declare martial law." In denying that her husband ever hurt anyone, Imelda Marcos insisted that Psinakis—not she—ought to be tried as a terrorist.

Ade Domingo was, perhaps, the star witness for the prosecution, testifying that Baruso repeatedly asked her to spy on her own son and everyone else in the KDP. She said Baruso often called Silme and Gene "Mao Maos."

Expert witnesses for the plaintiffs poured in from all over the country. Richard Falk, a political science professor from Princeton

166

University, testified that Silme and Gene fit exactly the pattern of people Marcos typically targeted for harassment and injury. Falk attacked the assertion made repeatedly by Hibey, that these two activists were beneath the grandeur of Marcos's wrath.

One expert witness after another pointed out what had been obvious to many during the Reagan years: Marcos was a bully. He had rarely killed an aristocrat, though he might have harassed his or her family. Someone as influential and popular as Ninoy Aquino made Marcos terribly apprehensive. He left Aquino in jail for years, afraid to eliminate him until 1983, when his regime was crumbling so palpably that the murder resulted from panic as much as anything else.

In 1983, Ninoy Aquino, the first powerful figure Marcos had ever taken on, was well prepared. "The act of my returning to Manila is victory in itself." He put on a bulletproof vest and made sure the press was covering him right up to his terrifying, most public end. No one believed Marcos's explanation of the assassination, though he rarely murdered people with power, so effective was he at bullying fall guys, innocents, thousands of people who couldn't fight back. Marcos took on Silme Domingo and Gene Viernes because they looked like little guys, only union people. Marcos knew that if labor unions in the Philippines became stronger, the price of exports would rise and a source of cheap labor would dry up. Fewer people would leave the Philippines, if they were paid a living wage. Silme and Gene fit the profiles of Marcos's victims perfectly, but joined with their families and friends, they were terribly big.

❖

Bonifacio Gillego, now a representative in his home country, appeared on the stand in a pinstripe suit, polished and unshakeable, making it clear to the jury that he had been CIA-trained. According to him, at least four and as many as eight Philippine intelligence outfits operated in the United States, all receiving orders from Marcos and General Ver. Their job was to monitor and operate against any and all anti-Marcos forces. "Rather than gather legitimate intelligence aimed at preserving the national security of the Philippine government," Gillego testified, "most of Marcos's intelligence efforts were aimed at counteracting and neutralizing the influence of anti-Marcos organizations who sought to expose the repressive nature of the Marcos regime, aid the opposition in the Phillipines, and influence American public opinion against continued US aid and support of the regime."

When Gillego spoke, the jury was riveted, the man in the flannel shirt still nodding empathetically as Gillego named military spies and agents in the US who operated under benign titles such as "cultural attaché" and "financial advisor," working with influential Filipinos known as "assets" to spy upon anti-Marcos activities in the US.

Silme and Gene, Gillego pointed out, were definitely people Marcos would have moved on; with the passing of the Hawaiian resolution, labor forces sympathetic to workers in the Philippines could have encouraged a large number of shipping strikes. The propaganda costs, alone, of reporting on the oppression of labor in the Philippines was beyond reckoning.

While on the stand, Gillego also acknowledged it was he who had discovered that the financial records for the phony Mabuhay Corporation, Malabed's propaganda machine, included an unexplained $15,000 expenditure on May 17, 1981. This was the same day Tony Baruso was supposed to have been in San Francisco, conferring with Malabed about hiring Gene and Silme's killers. Gillego remained calm under cross-examination, repeating every statement with confidence, sometimes adding words to give his testimony greater weight. When Hibey finally let him go, several members of the victims' families felt as if a meteorite had just opened a fissure in the earth beneath the courthouse.

The men and women of the jury sat with heads bowed, as though understanding for the first time that, though few in number, they had the power, the responsibility, to rule against a corrupt head of state for murder.

❋

In late November, the lawyers for the plaintiff, the victims' families, were moving towards closing arguments. Their hardest job still remained: to prove the monetary worth of what had been lost with their comrades' deaths. Because the expert witness they had wanted to testify to establish Silme's "worth" was not available, Terri Mast was forced to perform the difficult task of assessing her dead husband, both as a partner-householder and father.

Terri's voice shook so when she took the stand that Mike Withey had to repeat his questions to get her answers heard. When asked to repeat their actual salaries as union representatives in 1981, one or two jury members laughed. Granted, the figures were eight years old, but Terri also had to laugh from the witness stand. The attorney smiled ironically to the bench. Everyone in the courtroom realized at once that those organizers had worked for a motive other than money.

Then, suddenly, the ice was broken and melted by a blast meant to burn deep. Withey moved to his table and came back holding two poster-sized photos of Silme with his two little girls. There was Silme, big as life, holding Ligaya and Kaalyan to his chest as though he would never let them go. Many in the room had never seen his face, his warm, wide smile, until that moment.

The course of the morning was changed utterly. The ploy wasn't all that surprising; earlier in the trial, Withey had raised up a life-sized photo of Gene lying on the floor of the union hall, awash in his own blood. Dave Della, first to find Gene, had been on the stand at the time. Slumping down in his chair, Della looked for a moment as if he might pass out. Not telling the witness about the picture was part of the strategy. Della's reaction was as strong as if he had said, "Never claim Gene Viernes died instantly. Look at the pain and suffering of the one who came upon him—too late."

Now Withey raised the picture of Silme, alive with his children, and turned to the jury. "What price the loss of a father? How much is it worth to daughters to have a father of this caliber miss their first dates, their proms, their driving lessons, bringing home their first serious friends, getting married?" By the time he finished talking, the sound of quiet weeping filled the courtroom.

It was a fine strategy: get the jury to feel Terri's loathing for being forced to say that a husband dead might be worth more in one lump sum than his paychecks spread over a lifetime; drive these facts home in a painfully domestic manner, so emotionally charged that the other side feels the heat. Then raise that photo.

❦

The final argument for the defense was predictable. Hibey's plea that the Marcoses were immune as former heads of state sounded pathetic, a melodramatic note from an old Nixon thriller in which US national security was constantly being threatened. His more immediate argument was even sadder. "Some witnesses gave you the perception that monitoring and surveillance is harassment and intimidation. Governments monitor and surveil and it is legal to do so." The jury no doubt already knew this; to be reminded of a venal government's excesses was not the defense's best tactic. Baruso's and Malabed's attorneys wanted the judge to determine against or, possibly, for them in a separate ruling after the verdict came in, which sounded like a plea for mercy.

Prior to this, Malabed's attorney, Kate Alfieri, had asked the jury to believe that Malabed and Baruso had not met in May 1981, just prior to the murders; therefore, the crucial exchange of monies could never have happened. The families' attorneys had immediately produced a witness who claimed that Baruso and Malabed often met at Dimas Alang conferences, and that he had seen them at lunch together on the day the Mabuhay books indicated an ambiguous $15,000 payout.

This was an embarrassing closing argument to give a jury asked to deliver a verdict regarding conspiracy to murder and civil damages to be calculated as a result of this prolonged crime. People in that courtroom could not help but wonder at the coldness of the other side. Or perhaps they understood in that moment that there are people willing to murder the spirit of an entire class. Withey insisted that the evidence revealed "some of the most outrageous acts a foreign government has inflicted upon American citizens."

"When the next millennium arrives in the year 2000," Withey summed up, "and history finally writes the look back at the Marcos regime, perhaps we can all hope that the end of repression and the value of human rights will be established. And when that history is written, there will be a small footnote, maybe even a paragraph, about a case tried in Seattle, Washington ... and that paragraph will say that justice was done, a light was lit for freedom. It will say in the words of the Old Testament, 'May justice flow like water and may righteousness come down like a mighty stream.'"

As Withey concluded, the Viernes and Domingo families had all they could do to keep from leaping from their seats with clenched fists raised. The jury filed out. The foreman, the bearded man in the flannel shirt, looked grim and ashen, but determined.

Terri pictured Silme and Gene framing the elderly, smiling Filipino. Let's make them real, she prayed. Ade and Cindy, too, wanted to bring Silme and Gene out of history, to assure they were not relegated in time to being martyrs or statues or poster-sized photos. Bring them out, finally, as equal to truth; make their history dynamic.

Although it was only a brief time before the jury filed back in with the verdict, people in the courtroom grew so overwrought they could scarcely sit still. Judge Rothstein held the slip of paper and repeated the questions put to the jurors.

"Was any defendant a member of a conspiracy?" She looked toward the Domingo and Viernes families. "For defendant Ferdinand Marcos, yes. For defendant Imelda Marcos, yes."

The spectators sat motionless, stunned, as if they could not believe their ears. "Were the murders an overt act of this conspiracy? For Silme Domingo, yes. For Gene Viernes, yes."

The plaintiffs won on every count. The judgement awarded over $15 million in damages: $12 million to the children of Silme Domingo and Terri Mast and over $3 million to Barbara Viernes, Gene's sister.

As Rothstein continued to read the jury's determinations, sobs broke out all over the room. Attorneys Jim Douglas and Mike Withey, who had remained contained and assured throughout the trial, put their faces down on the table and wept uninhibitedly, as though eight years of emotion had just burst through a dam, a torrent of realized justice.

As the judge and jury left the courtroom, a joyous pandemonium broke out. Mike Withey and Cindy Domingo rocked in each other's arms, weeping and shouting, "We made it! We made it!"

Terri, her arm around Ade's shoulders, called over the noise to a clutch of reporters, "This is exactly what we wanted! We put on the best case we possibly could—and we won!"

Postcript
Seattle
1994

Ferdinand Marcos died an exile in Hawaii in September 1989. His body was returned for burial in the Philippines on September 10, 1993. In March 1991, Tony Baruso was charged with aggravated murder. A month later he was convicted, sentenced to life without parole. The jury found him guilty of conspiring to murder Gene Viernes, but not Silme Domingo. Silme's death was determined to be the result of his being with Gene when the gunmen entered the union hall. Their motive behind shooting Silme was merely to silence him, the jury determined. On September 23, 1993, Imelda Marcos was convicted of corruption by a Philippine court and sentenced to nine to twelve years imprisonment for each of two counts.

171

BIBLIOGRAPHICAL SOURCES

Raymond Bonner, Waltzing with a Dictator, The Marcoses and the Making of American Policy, Times Books (New York), 1987.

Taylor Branch and Eugene Proper, Labyrinth, Viking (New York), 1982.

Walter Karp, The Politics of War: the Story of Two Wars which Altered Forever the Political Life of the American Republic 1890-1920 Harper & Row (New York), 1979.

Stanley Karnow, In Our Image: America's Empire in the Philippines, Random House (New York), 1989.

Philippines, APA Publications (Singapore), 1989.

1950 Yearbook of Local 37, the Inland Boatman Union (Seattle).

Resolution of Local 37 of the ILWU, Honolulu, Hawaii, April, 1981.

Articles concerning the Domingo-Viernes case, appearing in the *Seattle Times*, *Seattle Post-Intelligencer*, *International Examiner*, *Seattle Sun*, and *ang Katipinan*, 1981 through 1993. Articles by Gene Viernes on Pacific Northwest cannery history, appearing in *International Examiner*, late 1970s.

Interviews, as indicated in the Acknowledgments section.

Transcripts of the US District Court, Western District of Washington at Seattle. Estate of Silme Domingo and Gene Viernes, plaintiffs vs. Ferdinand Marcos, et al, defendants, November 28, 1989. Transcripts of the Superior Court of Washington, County of King. State of Washington, plaintiff, vs. Fortunado L. Dictado, defendant, May 6, 1982. Transcripts of the Superior Court of Washington, etc., State of Washington (plaintiff), vs. Jimmy Ramil and Pompeyo Guloy Jr. (defendants).

"I want the Wide American Earth" by Carlos Bulosan is from the Carlos Bulosan Papers reprinted with the permission of the University of Washington Libraries.

p.50
"A Sorry Freedom by Nazim Hikmet, from Poems of Nazim Hikmet translated by Randy Blasing and Mutlu Konuk, Copyright © 1994 by Randy Blasing and Mutlu Konik. Reprinted by permission of Persea Books.

p.125
"Profits Enslave the World" was published in *Philip Vera Cruz: A Personal History of Filipino Immigrants and the Farmworkers Movement* by Craig Scharlin and Lilia Villanueva, Copyright © 1992, The Regents of the University of California. Reprinted with the permission of the UCLA Asian American Studies Center and the UCLA Labor Center.

INDEX

173

The body of this book was set in 10/12 point Revival565BT
and the Library of Congress Cataloging-in-Publication
information in Moderne.